PRAISE FOR THE AUTHOR AND
Identity Marketing™

"*Identity Marketing* was a refreshing reframe to how we are looking at marketing. Consumers are bombarded with noise and endless pitches, and the Identity Marketing framework cuts through all of that by focusing on building a brand that resonates deeply with the audience."

— JEN BUTLER
Marketing Leader

"V is very good at making sure information is easy to understand while still being high level. *Identity Marketing* is so fresh, insightful, thought provoking, fun, and instantly useful. My entire team is empowered to share and contribute which helped everyone to take ownership and feel like a part of the movement"

— SARA WALKA
Small Business Owner

"Seriously, if you're stuck trying to figure out how to position your brand and build your personal team, you NEED *Identity Marketing!*"

— JENNY LEAVITT
Marketer

"It was simply amazing to be able to not only work through those concepts on *Identity Marketing* but also put all that into immediate action. I just felt like my brain was exploding with "aha" moments as the puzzle pieces were falling into place."

— NAOMIE HARRIS
Marketer

"Getting so much clarity on why my marketing wasn't landing in the way I know it should. Defining different identity stages for my ideal customer along her journey of becoming was a game changer!"

— DR. JORDIN WIGGINS
Naturopathic Doctor and Feminine Burnout & Intimacy Coach

"I am so impressed with the ways that Veronica was able to get us thinking differently about marketing and generating so many amazing ideas!"

— JESSICA BLAKE
Operations Manager

Copyright © 2025 Veronica Romney

All Rights Reserved. No part of this publication may be reproduced, stored in or introduced into a retrieval system, or transmitted, in any form or by any means (electronic, mechanical, photocopying, recording, or otherwise), without the prior written permission of both the copyright owner and the publisher of this book.

The scanning, uploading, and distribution of this book via the Internet or via any other means without the persmission of the publisher is illegal and punishable by law. Please purchase only authorized electronic editions and do not participate in or encourage eloctronic piracy of copyrightable materials. Your support of the author's rights is appreciated.

All materials, including trademarks or copyrights, mentioned in the book belong to their respective owners. Any reference to third-party trademarks is for informational or educational purposes only and does not imply any affiliation, sponsorship, or endorsement by the trademark owner. This material does not guarantee any particular results. The information provided is intended for general guidance and educational purposes only. Any financial, business, or legal outcomes depend on various factors, including individual effort, market conditions, and unique circumstances. No guarantees are made regarding specific outcomes or earnings. Always consult with a professional for advice tailored to your specific needs.

ISBN: 979-8-218-55673-0
Library of Congress Control Number: 2024927229

Printed and Distributed by IngramSpark in the United States
Edited by Jill Garvin Durkin
Co-written with Emily Conley
Designed and Illustrated by Heather Terwilliger

Published by Veronica Romney in the United States,
1457 Kelly Road #114, Apex, NC, 27502

www.veronicaromney.com

Identity Marketing

*How to Create Loyal, Lifelong
Fans and a Legendary Brand*

(No Matter What You Sell or the Size of Your Budget)

Veronica Romney

To my parents, my family, and my team—the people who shaped my identity.

Table *of* Contents

Foreword	14
Introduction	18

START HERE:
BRINGING IDENTITY MARKETING TO LIFE

Customize Your Reading Experience	32
Your Identity Marketing Playlist	34
Next-Level Integration	36

PART ONE:
IDENTITY MARKETING

Ch 1	What is Identity Marketing?	42
Ch 2	Identity Marketing vs. Brand Identity	48
Ch 3	The Cure for Your Consumer's Crisis	54
Ch 4	A Better Way to Market and Sell	68

PART TWO:
THE UNDENIABLE POWER OF IDENTITY MARKETING

Ch 5	Resuscitating Brands and Companies *Featuring Barbie*	80
Ch 6	Tapping Into Unprecedented Market Share *Featuring Taylor Swift, NFL, Red Bull, GoPro*	94
Ch 7	Developing A Cultlike Following *Featuring Dallas Cowboys Cheerleaders, Russell Brunson's Funnel Hackers*	108

Ch 8   Disrupting Saturated Markets With Cause   120
Featuring SMASHD's Nicole the Intern, Presidents Trump and Reagan

Ch 9   Transforming Intangibles Into Ridiculously Profitable Tangibles   136
Featuring Nike, Red Ants Pants, The Pink Bee

PART THREE:

HOW TO CREATE LOYAL, LIFELONG FANS AND A LEGENDARY BRAND *(NO MATTER WHAT YOU SELL OR THE SIZE OF YOUR BUDGET)*

Ch 10   The Identity Code   148
How to use an easy 4-step framework to unlock a marketable identity

Ch 11   Find It   154
How to secret shop yourself without spending millions

Ch 12   Prove It   168
How to get immediate buy-in without outdated focus groups

Ch 13   Name It   182
How to give your identity deep meaning without surface-level gimmicks

Ch 14   Dress It   200
How to make your identity feel real

Identity Marketing Legends   218

PART FOUR:

LEVERAGING IDENTITY BEYOND MARKETING AND SALES

Ch 15	The Cure for Your Labor Force Crisis *How to attract and retain the best talent without expensive benefits or massive signing bonuses*	238
Ch 16	Identity-Based Leadership *How to improve your leadership without investing another dollar in professional development*	246
Ch 17	The Identity-Based Team *How to give your team a competitive edge without coercion, fear, or monetary rewards*	260
Ch 18	The Identity-Based Organization *How to build a strong, passionate culture without being cheesy or lame*	270

Conclusion and Invitation	278
Additional Resources	282
Acknowledgments	284
About the Author	288
Notes	290

Foreword

When you work with Veronica Romney, you're not just a contractor or an employee. You become a different person—a better, more confident, empowered person, with a deep belief in your capabilities and potential.

When you work with Veronica Romney, you become part of the V-hive.

We started calling ourselves the V-hive as a nod to V's powerful, spicy "Veyoncé" personality and our collective identity as the ones who got to buzz around and help execute her vision.

At first, she wasn't so sure about the name, but we kept using it and it stuck.

When she asked us, her team—her V-hive—to collectively write the foreword for this book, we had to double-check that we'd heard her right.

She could have asked any number of the renowned industry and thought leaders she is connected with to write an impressive summary of who she is and why you should trust her brilliant theories and framework.

But she insisted she wanted us to describe her as a leader. So we channeled our inner writers and turned to good old Google to give us the word or phrase that would sum up her leadership.

We found positive leadership descriptions like coaching, servant, transformational, and visionary, which are great ... but not expansive or accurate enough.

So, we made a list of the words that came to mind when we think about who V is and how she shows up as a leader.

- *Compassionate*
- *Genuine*
- *Collaborative*
- *Charismatic*
- *Professional*
- *Inspirational*
- *Impressive*

Again—all accurate. But not enough.

As we all compared stories about how we'd met V, what we were like when we started working with her, and where we all are now ... one thing became very clear. V doesn't just lead her team. She finds the unique greatness that is in each of us and empowers us to be our biggest, best selves.

We each have a different story with a remarkably similar thread running strong through our individual experiences—we are more confident, more bold, and more successful now than we ever could have dreamed of being before working with V.

V leads by recognizing the magic in each of her team members, calling out the greatness *she* sees, and consistently creating opportunities for us to use our gifts and see ourselves the way she sees us.

Being in V's orbit awakened the gifts and true potential that lay dormant in each of us—squashed down and silenced for different reasons and through different experiences. She brought our magic to life by first *recognizing* it and then championing it, making it impossible for us to not see what she sees when she looks at us.

We each had a story about how being part of the V-hive had irrevocably changed us. From leaving toxic work environments where we were silenced and taken advantage of to learning how to speak up and be confident in our skills and expertise, to raising our own prices, and finding the courage to strike out and do what we really wanted to do—becoming part of the V-hive had changed our very identities.

It's impossible to play small and stay hidden when you're on V's team.

She makes us laugh (a lot), she impresses us daily, and she inspires the deepest levels of loyalty. Once you're in the V-hive, you're part of the team for life—no matter where your big goals and dreams take you. And to be perfectly honest, there's nowhere we would rather be.

We didn't realize why V wanted us to write her introduction until after we had done it. In true Veronica fashion, she knew all along how deeply connected our identity as the V-hive was and how becoming a team had changed us. She just wanted us to figure it out for ourselves.

Leadership at its finest, if you ask us.

With love and gratitude,

THE V-Hive ♥

Introduction

I'm not a writer.

At least, I didn't identify as one.

And yet, I've spent an obscene amount of time and money investing in the tools, education, and support to become one so I can put this book in your hands.

And that right there, my new friends, is the point of this entire book:

> The wallet achieves what the mind believes.

In the chapters that follow, I'm going to teach you all about Identity Marketing™—what it is, why it matters, and how you can use it to level up your own marketing and sales. But first, I need to introduce myself and give you a little background about why exactly you should trust me—an entrepreneur, speaker, wife, mother, leader, and marketer.

And if we haven't met yet, I'm Veronica. But

my friends call me V, so please feel free to do so too.

Everything you need to know about my expertise, knowledge, and perspective is encapsulated in the different parts of my identity.

Who I am = what I do.

Peel back the layers of my identity, and you'll see how all of who I am and what I've learned as a consequence is for your gain—not mine. My sole purpose in writing this book is to help you market your brilliance and make a significant impact in your own businesses, careers, and life.

Ready to explore the different identities of the *real* V?

Warning: It may cause you to reflect upon your own identity, which is deep for a book introduction.

I AM AN ENTREPRENEUR.

I have chased down every certification out there and poured more money than I care to count into professional development, menI have chased down every certification out there and poured more money than I care to count into professional development, mentorship, business masterminds, and coaching to become the entrepreneur I am today.

My Cuban-immigrant parents owned an HVAC (heating ventilation and air conditioning) company for over three decades, so I feel like entrepreneurship was always in my blood. I knew this particular ocean would eventually call to me, I just didn't know when.

But nothing prepares you f'or this world like actually diving into it.

Through all the iterations my work has taken, leading my team and working together to execute my vision has been some of the most rewarding work I've ever done.

To be a successful entrepreneur, you must not only be willing to fail (and fail, and fail, and fail)—but you must be willing to learn from each failure so you go on to make new mistakes instead of repeating the same ones.

Because I identify as an entrepreneur, I pour my time, money, and energy into mentors, technology, and service providers who support my growth and success.

I AM A KEYNOTE SPEAKER.

I've been speaking in breakout rooms for years,

teaching groups of professionals how to avoid the top three *A,B, and C* mistakes or implement these five strategies for more *X,Y, and Z*. I was comfortable in this position and was often invited to be a guest or expert speaker at events, conferences, and private masterminds. But when I decided I wanted to level up and become a *keynote speaker*, I had to completely change how I saw myself.

I started by doing what I do best: investing in professionals to mentor and teach me. I'm still a work in progress, as all great speakers will tell you. You will still often find me running on my treadmill while I watch my speaking heroes deliver their keynote for the fourteenth time on YouTube.

And it's all worth it.

To stand on that stage and not tell people what to do, but *how to think*, to create dramatic, game-changing shifts in how they view their work and get results ... it's fulfilling in a new, beautiful way.

Because I identify as an international keynote speaker, I follow impressive speakers, pay attention to who is hosting and attending can't-miss events, and pay for the support and education I need to improve my own speaking skills and connections.

I AM A WIFE.

There's a saying about marriage that I've heard over the years that I've loved since the first time I heard it: "Become someone you'd want to marry."

And somehow, by absolute heavenly design, I met a man— in a *questionable* club in downtown Salt Lake City at twenty years old—who fulfills that expression every day in our own marriage.

Yes, I am a strong female who challenges conventional wisdom on the regular and carves out her own way forward, but that doesn't mean I wear more than the proverbial fifty percent of the marital pants.

As a wife, I don't want my husband to be anything but his highest self. And I hold myself to the same standards.

What's truly beautiful in our partnership is that by knowing myself, I've helped *him* know himself and step into his own power.

And together, we are each able to pursue our individual dreams, achieve next-level joint success, and feel supported every step of the way.

Because I identify as a wife, I consider how every choice I make impacts my partner. I put my time and money into not just advancing my own needs, but into making sure my husband is supported in all of his needs and interests, too. Our marriage is where I first learned what being on a dream team really means.

I AM A MOTHER.

Which means I'm more terrified of ruining my kids than I am of anything else in life.

Ruining my business? Suck.

Ruining my marriage? Heartbreaking.

But ruining my kids? *Unforgivable.*

The good news is that I'm pretty sure if you're as concerned about ruining your kids as I am, we won't in the end.

When I was pregnant, I was constantly aware of what stage of growth and development my boys were at—grape, lemon, watermelon. I knew.

And since they were born, I've remained vigilant.

We pour *a lot* of money, time, and attention into those two little man cubs—giving them everything we can, from the best education and sports training, to therapy and family-first vacations. I want them to have the life skills and emotional intelligence they need alongside the education and athletic prowess they're developing.

If I'm doing anything right with my kids, it's showing up as their relentless number one fan.

I cheer them on in everything they do. I want to pour so much confidence, respect, and self-belief into them that I can dare the world to *try* and to rob them of it. Because as all parents know, it will try.

Because I identify as a mother, I make life decisions, big and small, based on what is best for my children. I prioritize our family's connection and experiences over practically anything else.

I AM A LEADER.

Most people grow up expecting to be a partner or a parent ... but I grew up knowing in my core that I was meant for more than just those two core identities.

Like one of my favorite Disney characters, Moana, I was always aware of the "calling" – —I just didn't know when my "ocean" would call exactly.

Because I identify as a visionary, I followed my life's calling even when it led me in unexpected or challenging directions.

Speaking of Moana, there's a song she sings with her grandmother, "Song of the Ancestors", that speaks deeply to how I feel about my life's calling.

In the song, Moana's grandmother describes the girl she knows, who loves her home and her family. As she continues to describe this girl, she advises her that life will be hard sometimes, but that those struggles will reveal who she is and what she's meant to do with her life.

She cautions Moana to listen to the quiet voice inside her and not to let anything on earth silence the whisper she hears in her heart.

Moana does know who she is, and she responds by affirming what her grandmother has seen in her, accepting and embracing the calling she feels deep in her soul.

In the movie, Moana feels called to the sea, even though she's from an island of people who never venture off the island.

She thanks her grandmother for her wisdom, ensuring her that she knows who she is. She knows her calling, and she knows what she must do.

I feel this, like Moana, deep in my soul.

And no matter what happens, I know who

I am ... I am Veronica—the daughter of Cuban immigrants, the wife of an incredible partner, the mother to the most wonderful sons, proud entrepreneur and team leader, powerful keynote speaker, relentless visionary leader.

And each of the identities I've shared with you so far? I've wrestled with ALL of them. Wondering if I was doing the right thing, doubting my skills, hoping I was enough.

I've spent more restless nights than I can count, struggling with self-doubt.

I've survived mortifying outer body moments of "What did I just say?!" and "I can't believe I *did* that!"

You can't possibly KNOW yourself without truly wrestling with your identity in the depths of your soul—asking yourself, "Who am I? No... who am I *really*?"

And yet, there's one identity that I've never doubted or questioned.

I AM A MARKETER.

All of my identities coalesce into one cohesive entity as a Marketer.

This is incredible, considering I accidentally fell into marketing, through an internship in college (I wanted a spot on the finance team, but they only had openings in marketing) and discovered how much I loved it. Not only was it fun, creative, and energizing ... it felt natural. Like breathing.

I returned to my university classes, getting sober-drunk off the strategies, terminology, and history I was learning in my marketing classes.

Consumer behavior? *Give me more.*

Churn rate? *Tell me everything.*

Customer acquisition rate? *I'm obsessed.*

I have been in a faithful, committed relationship with my identity and a committed professional as a marketer since I was nineteen years old, and I have never wavered.

I can't *unsee* the world without a constant marketing lens.

Which means I also see all people as marketers.

Yes, *you too* are a marketer, whether you have a marketing diploma hanging above your desk like I do, or you've never thought twice about marketing.

CEO or business owner? *Marketer.*

Busy mom? *Marketer.*

Curious student? *Marketer.*

Marketing is the art and science of ethically persuading someone to say *yes* to us in some capacity.

Whether that persuasion is for selling a good or service, getting your picky toddler to eat their dinner, convincing the PTA to fund an after-school program, or talking your partner into taking that vacation you've been dreaming about, you are *constantly* marketing yourself and your ideas.

So yes, I one hundred percent own my identity as a Marketer. And you should too.

This book is critical for *all* because we are *all* Marketers.

Turns out, customers are having the same identity crisis—asking themselves the very questions I asked myself: "Who *am* I?"

When you identify as a marketer, the way you show up in life changes. You view the world with marketer's eyes, constantly looking for ways to persuade others to take the actions you know they need to take. You're seeking out opportunities to invest your money wisely, in who you are and who you want to be.

Identifying as a marketer means always thinking about how to help customers answer that those pressing questions of "Who am I?" and "Who do I want to be?"

Because you identify as a marketer, you put your money where it will make the biggest difference. And that's why you're here, holding this book. You are facing your new, confirmed, or reaffirmed identity as a marketer.

And I am so honored to sing my own (marketing) "Song of the Ancestors" to show you the way—to lifelong brand loyalty, advocacy, and eternal affinity.

What do you say? Are you ready to tap into your inner Moana and answer the call of better marketing with me?

START HERE:

Bringing Identity Marketing to Life

Don't read every word or chapter in this book.

Yes, I'm the author telling you not to read every single word of this book.

Why?

Because I'm doing you a solid from a place of consideration and personal experience.

Here are the facts*:

- About **20% of nonfiction books (including business books)** are never opened after purchase.
- Studies indicate that only 30 - 40% of physical books purchased are fully read.
- Business books often fall into the "partially read" category, with readers skimming for key takeaways rather than reading cover to cover.

These stats accurately reflect my own experience if you were to peep the bookshelves of unread marketing, sales, and business strategy books behind me in my own office. But here's the thing:

I don't want you to read this book.

CUSTOMIZE YOUR READING EXPERIENCE | 33

I want you to *apply* its teachings.

To help you do that, we've created a quiz to **give you a customized reading experience with your own "cheat sheet,"** outlining the specific chapters and stories you'll benefit most from!

You answer a few questions, and we'll tell you what to skip and where to be laser-focused so you can be ruthlessly efficient and wildly effective with your reading and immediate marketing efforts.

Consider this your *Customized Identity Marketing CliffsNotes.*

I got you, friend.

identitymarketingbook.com

Scan this code to access the quiz

*According to sources from Jellybooks Ltd and Nikola Roza.

It's Time To Access Your Own Identity Marketing Identity

What do The Rock, Beyoncé, and Kobe Bryant have in common?

One powerful playlist that fuels their identity transformations.

Dwayne Johnson → **The Rock**
Listens to "Enter Sandman" by Metallica and "Till I Collapse" by Eminem.

Beyoncé → **Sasha Fierce**
Streams her own hits like "Run the World (Girls)" and "Formation."

Kobe → **Black Mamba**
A fascinating mix of hip-hop ("All of the Lights" by Kanye West) and classical music (Beethoven's "Moonlight Sonata") got Kobe ready to take on his opponents.

Those transformations all start with specific

songs and pumped-up playlists that channel the energy and vibes they need to crush it in their fields.

And now YOU have your own Identity Marketing Identity Playlist!

You → **Identity Marketing Legend**

We channeled the energy and next-level vibes that define Identity Marketing into a perfect playlist, and we're sharing it with you!

Download this Spotify playlist and tune in when you need to assume your marketing alter ego and create lifelong, loyal fans and a legendary brand.

Warning: This playlist's energy is HIGH and may incite dancing, fist-pumping, or wild, erratic movements. Proceed with caution.

identitymarketingbook.com

Scan this code to access the playlist

Bringing Identity Marketing to Life *for* Your Brand and Business

Next-Level Integration

Before you officially get started on your Identity Marketing journey, we want you to know that this isn't *just* a book.

Our team works with real brands, CEOs, marketers, teams, and business owners every day to turn the things they learn here into a real, marketable strategy, and we have an entire website dedicated to giving you resources and guidance to make sure reading this book leads directly to action.

Knowledge isn't enough. It's what you do with your knowledge that moves the needle and makes an impact.

Here are some of the ways we can bring Identity Marketing to life with you:

FREE IDENTITY MARKETING EXPERIENCE

This live training session brings the Identity Marketing™ framework to life in under an hour. Author Veronica Romney, will show you how to apply the key principles of the book to your brand and answer your burning questions in real-time. Master the methods of the book before you even finish reading it!

thisisidentitymarketing.com

IDENTITY MARKETING ON STAGE

Take your event to the next level with a keynote that redefines how your audience sees marketing and their role in it. Keynote speaker, Veronica Romney, will take your group on a journey to discover the power of shifting from selling products to helping customers align with a deeper identity.

Every talk is customized to your industry, packed with real-world examples, and delivered with energy and actionable insights. Let's empower your audience to create brands that people don't just buy from—they forever belong to.

More about keynote opportunities here:
veronicaromney.com

IDENTITY MARKETING INTENSIVE

In just two days, uncover your brand's marketable identity and bring it to life in this unique paid workshop. On Day 1, you'll find and validate your identity with confidence. On Day 2, you'll deepen its meaning and personify it for maximum impact.

Whether you attend solo or with your team, you'll be supported every step of the way; through curated breakout rooms, intentional collaboration, and expert coaches to ensure everyone experiences a breakthrough. This is your chance to master the 4-step Identity Code™ framework and forever shift your marketing from "buy this" to "be this."

More about the Intensive here:
youridentitymarketing.com

Your brand's lifelong, loyal fans are out there looking for you. We're here to help you leverage the influence of Taylor Swift, the success of Barbie, and the longevity of Harley Davidson ... without fame, a massive budget, or a century-long tenure.

You in?

PART ONE:

Identity Marketing

CHAPTER ONE

What is Identity Marketing?
A Brand Strong Enough to Be Buried In.

The lid of the beautiful, shiny black coffin closed, revealing a massive Harley Davidson logo emblazoned on one man's eternal resting place. The man being buried, Gary, was a big personality known for his love and embodiment of Harley Davidson.

He met the woman who would become his wife when she stopped to admire his bike, and picked her up with a smooth line about needing her number. He spent his days as a Harley H.O.G. (Harley Owner's Group) member—riding, taking care of his bike, hanging out with other H.O.G. members, and talking about riding.

When I asked Gary's step-granddaughter, Nicole Case, if he had specifically requested that he be buried in a Harley Davidson-branded casket, in his riding leathers, she couldn't remember the exact nature of his requests, but confidently shared, "Even if he hadn't specified this ... it's what we would have done as a family."

Because that's who Gary *was*.

His identity was inextricably linked to Harley Davidson. He was and continues to be eternally a Harley Hog. His beloved "hog" motorcycle was handed down as a treasured heirloom to his son after Gary passed: a tangible way for Gary's spirit to live on in the brand that defined him.

Gary isn't the only man buried in a Harley Davidson-branded casket. While exact stats are hard to come by, according to the caskets and services available across the country, other Harley Hogs have the option of being laid to rest in an official Harley Davidson-emblazoneed casket, proudly displaying the logo that defined them in life and continues with them into eternity or even carried to their final resting place in a customized Harley Davidson Hearse.[1]

INTRODUCING: IDENTITY MARKETING™

A brand you'll be associated with for all of eternity? That's an affinity most brands can only dream of. Eternal brand affinity doesn't happen by accident. In fact, it doesn't happen at all for most brands.

It all comes down to one thing: Identity Marketing.

Identity Marketing isn't about the brand. It's about the consumer. It's about connecting your brand so deeply with your consumer's identity—who they are and who they want to be—that they *want* to be buried in your brand.

It's about shifting from marketing the outcomes and benefits of your brand, to marketing an invitation to become the person your customer wants to be.

Identity Marketing taps into an unmatched power source, built on a strategy of tailoring your marketing to resonate with the personal identities of your consumers.

It requires you to understand and leverage your buyer's unique characteristics, values, and lifestyles, so you can craft messaging, create marketing strategies, and build a brand that either affirms your buyer's identity or embodies the identity your buyer aspires to.

Identity Marketing is the difference between a

brand people like and buy and a brand thousands of people request to be buried in.

AN ETERNAL IDENTITY

I will never forget sitting in a consumer behavior class as a college undergrad, nearly twenty years ago, and learning that people were regularly buried in Harley Davidson-branded caskets.

A lot of what I learned in that class amused me, but this particular business case study *fascinated* me.

Why?

Because I learned this fact while sitting in class at Brigham Young University, a Christian institution, where members of the devout Christian community are regularly buried with symbols of their faith.

And I think my newly formed marketing brain was alerted when I realized that a *brand* could have the same power as a *world religion*.

It was the first time I realized that a capitalistic identity could compete or even be on the same level as a godly identity.

Research has dated the earliest occurrences of humans being buried with personal tokens to about 120,000 years ago. In Qafzeh Cave in Israel, the remains of anatomically modern humans were found in 1934, buried with personal ornaments and tools—evidence that early humans were following deliberate burial practices and attached meaning to personal objects.[2]

It's no exaggeration to say people have been attempting to take things they love with them into the afterlife for over a hundred thousand years.

When you look at Harley Davidson, a brand that was founded in 1903, it's undeniably impressive that they have built an "eternal" brand that loyal customers choose to be buried with in just 120 years.

One man in Ohio spent eighteen years planning for and building a plexiglass box with his sons, where he would be eternally astride his beloved Harley.

When Billy Standley died at age 82, he was embalmed and set on his 1967 bike, sitting upright in the transparent case he'd built where he could rest for all eternity.

He'd bought three plots next to his wife's to make room for his "coffin," that would be placed inside an underground concrete vault large enough to contain it.

Standley said he didn't just want to ride his Harley Hog to heaven, he wanted the world to witness him do it.[3]

This is the power of Identity Marketing.

✓ KEY TAKEAWAYS

- Identity Marketing isn't about you—it's about your consumer. It's a powerful shift away from outcomes-based marketing.
- It's possible to build a strong enough identity that your customers take your brand to the grave.
- We've got a lot more to learn about Identity Marketing, so let's get to it!

CHAPTER TWO

Identity Marketing *vs.* Brand Identity

It's not what you look like ... it's who you are.

Most brands are so focused on building their own brand identity that they pass right by the power of Identity Marketing, not giving it another thought.

Brand identity is the set of unique characteristics that influence a brand's perceived personality, appearance, and behavior. It comes from the brand itself, in the intentional way the company wants the brand to be seen, recognized, and acknowledged by the public.

Brand identity focuses on what makes up your brand's image while Identity Marketing focuses on creating marketing that's customized to your target buyers' identity and aspirations.

Where brand identity is what your brand looks like externally, Identity Marketing is all about how your consumers identify internally.

And where brand identity gives you consistency across marketing channels and platforms, Identity Marketing is highly personalized and will adopt different marketing messages to tie in with different consumer identities.

There are a number of components that make up a brand's identity, including:

- Logos
- Typography
- Color palette
- Tagline
- Visual style
- Brand voice and tone

Your brand identity is how you stand out from your competitors. You need to look and sound different from the other companies selling the same things you are if you want to attract attention and buyers.

When you have a strong brand identity, you tend to build more brand recognition, loyalty, and trust.

Most companies build their brand identity around their target client or customer—figuring out how they want to appeal to a specific buyer so they can create messaging and marketing campaigns that speak to and attract that buyer.

And that worked—for a while.

But as Americus Reed II, Whitney M. Young Jr. professor of marketing at The Wharton School for over 24 years, so clearly points out in his *Handbook of Research on Identity Theory in Marketing*:

> *Brands are more than just logos and taglines. They are meaning systems. Products, services, organizations, behaviors or even people can be brands. That means that they are also markers of identity. Therefore the coupling of identity and marketing is a natural marriage.*

He goes on to define identity as "any category label to which a consumer self-associates either by choice or endowment."[4]

The consumer must choose to identify with an identity—it can't be forced on them or arbitrarily assigned.

Identity Marketing turns "selling" into building deep, meaningful connections with your buyers. It is the major shift from "buy this" to *be this*.

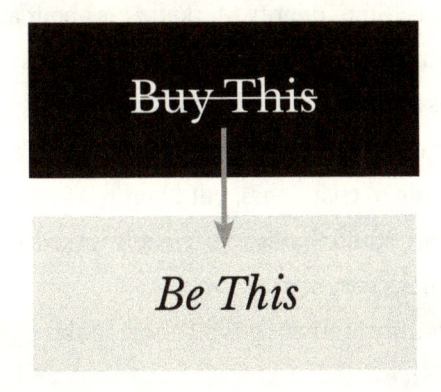

~~Buy This~~

Be This

The identity your brand cultivates with will be based on a core aspect of your customer's life:
- Profession—I am a lineman, teacher, CPA
- Life stage—I am a new mom, a DINK (double income no kids), retired
- Health and Wellness—I am vegan, a gym rat, a climber
- Hobbies—I am a writer, a cyclist, a sourdough aficionado
- Aspirations—I am wealthy, youthful, a homesteader
- Beliefs—I am Christian, an advocate, agnostic
- Political affiliations—I am liberal, republican, independent

The "meaning system" is the key to Identity Marketing that works.

It has to go deeper than convincing, persuading, or selling. Identity Marketing is about aligning your brand with the core of who your customer sees themselves as (or wants to be).

Brand identity can create a brand that's appealing to customers, but Identity Marketing creates a brand that is inextricably linked to your customer's very sense of self.

Identity Marketing is all about making your brand an extension of the lens through which your customer views themselves and the world. And it's the *only* way to build lifelong loyalty that extends to the grave.

✓ KEY TAKEAWAYS

- Brand identity is what your brand looks like.
- Identity Marketing is an intentional marketing strategy that aligns your brand with a core aspect of your customer's life and self-perception.
- Identity Marketing is the key to loyal, passionate buyers.

CHAPTER THREE

The Cure for Your Consumer's Crisis

"I've suffered from an identity crisis my entire life. It's why I went into acting."
—Matthew Rhys

You can make a lot of money without understanding who your customer is or what they want. For a while.

I worked with a husband-wife team who had started a business teaching people how to become Enneagram coaches. Their coaching model was simple and effective, and it was created in response to consumer demand.

As the personality tool they worked with gained popularity, their Instagram account grew to over 242,000 followers.

They used the revenue they generated from coaching course sales to create a website with an assessment tool that helped users figure out their enneagram number and results. This assessment brought in huge numbers of leads—up to 1,500 a day at the peak—and the company continued to grow.

They hired a robust team and created new products, wrote new books, did an entire book tour, and launched new offers as fast as they could create them.

Their revenue hit the multiple-seven-figure mark, and they turned up the volume even more. The co-founder found herself seriously ill and entirely burned out.

While one partner wanted to slow down, the other wanted to move even faster. They hired a COO (Chief Operating Officer) who hit the ground running at 100 mph, dragging the co-founder along at breakneck speed with one goal: create, create, create.

But while this exhausting pattern of massive offer creation and live launching was roaring along, sales were starting to decline. The business had an email list of over 150,000 people who weren't interested in buying what they were offering.

Finally, after a devastating launch that resulted in virtually no sales, the co-founder found herself demoralized, dejected, and ready to quit. After years of working ungodly hours and creating a massive collection of books, courses, and content, she felt stuck, lost, and without any desire to continue.

This is where I was invited to enter their story.

It was immediately clear to me that they had a huge misalignment in who they thought they were serving and who was actually in their audience. Their main lead generation tool was a personality assessment. The people taking this assessment were asking the question we're all asking: "Who am I?"

They didn't want to become coaches who taught others how to use this tool. They wanted to use the personality assessment to help them understand their own identity and inclinations.

The organization had essentially already sold to everyone in their audience who was interested in coaching, and they were left with hundreds of thousands of people who only wanted personal insight and growth, not a new career.

I recommended that the leaders lean into the personal aspect of the Enneagram that their audience was drawn to. I suggested they make a difficult pivot to meet their buyers where they were and invite them to become people who use the insights of their personality type to enrich and improve their lives.

But the founders saw their company as a coaching company. Despite the evidence, they insisted on maintaining their identity as a coaching company instead of shifting to meet their consumers' actual and desired identity. This refusal to align with their audience's identity left them with practically no incoming revenue. They were forced to lay off almost their entire team, and felt completely burned out and devastated.

A GLOBAL IDENTITY CRISIS

Who are you?

Where do you stand?

There's a huge, untapped market of consumers who are currently facing a massive identity crisis.

Within four years (2020 – 2024) we have collectively experienced:

- A worldwide pandemic that has resulted in over 7 million deaths to date
- Nationwide lockdowns and fear of the unknown with COVID-19

- Major inflation with soaring grocery prices
- Global housing crisis
- AI takeover
- A suffocating political atmosphere
- Mass layoffs

Where are we all left? Trying to figure out how to remain relevant amid all the upheaval and change. We've entered the era of the consumer rebrand. It's all about repositioning and revitalizing your brand in order to remain in the game and attract buyers' waning attention.

And guess what? Your customers are going through the same process themselves. They're trying to figure out who they are and what they care about, because nothing is the same as it was even five years ago.

So now you're desperately trying to rebrand and remain relevant to customers while simultaneously dealing with the fact that your ideal customer doesn't know who they are anymore.

Your customers, right now, are asking themselves "Who am I?" and "What do I stand for?"

> If your brand can offer a compelling answer to those questions, you've got legions of passionate consumers just waiting to become loyal, buying fans.

THE DECLINE OF OUTCOME-BASED MARKETING

According to the 2022 Edelman Trust Barometer, distrust has become society's default emotion. Other studies show that a whopping 96% of consumers sometimes actively seek out negative reviews.[5]

The more consumers are exposed to marketing strategies and techniques, the more they start to see through them.

The more information a typical consumer has, the less likely they are to believe unsubstantiated claims.

In a world full of fake news, everything gets lumped in together.

Your messaging, no matter how honest and authentic you try to be, is *perceived* by many of your target market as "fake news" or a sales tactic.

Consumers are growing more and more suspicious as we are consistently let down by leaders, led astray by the media, and subjected to non-stop information in the form of email, posts on X, TikToks, Instagram reels, and podcasts.

There is so much *noise* that instead of adjusting the volume and tuning out the nonsense, consumers are tuning out and disengaging with everything.

An erosion of trust, serious ad fatigue, and content saturation have all led us to the current abysmal consumer environment.

Your customers have given in to the fear-mongering and splurged on "silver bullet" solutions. They trusted brands and have been burned. They believed the hype and have been let down. Now they are jaded and skeptical of brands and sales tactics.

What worked a few years ago isn't cutting it today.

But *you* still need to make sales if you want to run a business or scale an organization.

WHAT IS AN AMBITIOUS LEADER, ASPIRING ENTREPRENEUR, OR NEW BUSINESS OWNER TO DO?

The truth is that brands have *never* been better positioned to seize greater market share and create a legion of passionate, committed customers. But it requires a new perspective on marketing.

Instead of getting mad about the state of the marketplace and wishing a downturn economy could flip a switch and start booming again, it's time to lean all the way in on a better way to connect with your customers. Time to build loyal, engaged fans, and create a standout brand.

It's time to shift from convincing your customers to *buy this*, to inviting them to *be this*.
It's time to embrace Identity Marketing.

HOW NOT TO DO IDENTITY MARKETING AND AVOID UNETHICAL TACTICS

Identity Marketing is powerful because it taps into the innate beliefs, passions, and perceptions of your consumer.

It's a powerful tool that must be wielded with caution, intention, and integrity. Because when

Identity Marketing goes off the rails—it can go seriously wrong.

When you lose your integrity and become solely focused on winning business, you put your customer in a precarious position.

Former clinical psychotherapist and current CEO of Kelly Ruta International, Kelly Ruta, outlined and highlighted specific unethical behaviors you should be on the look out for as a consumer and ensure you avoid as a marketer in a podcast interview for the Rainmaker Podcast in the fall of 2024.

1. Unethical brands use emotional manipulation.

Ruta says this happens when the business or coach blames the customer for their lack of results regardless of the actual effort the customer exerted: "You didn't get the results because you didn't work hard enough. And by the way, you need to be in my next-level program because clearly the lower level program is not for you."

While a small level of FOMO [fear of missing out] is normal and to be expected, emotional manipulators take it to a whole new level, leaving the customer with a deep belief that if they leave, opt out, or don't buy into what's being offered it will cause them harm and come with significant loss.

2. Unethical brands gaslight customers who complain.

Gaslighting happens when a customer comes forward with a legitimate complaint or issue and is told that the issue does not exist and their complaint is not valid.

3. Unethical brands do not accept criticism of any kind.

Mistakes are a natural, normal part of business. An ethical brand will acknowledge their mistakes and own their shortcomings.

But with an unethical brand: "We see the face of the brand being completely intolerant of criticism. They delete comments they don't want to have to respond to. They take posts down to control the narrative of the group. They pull their video down, but not because they want to replace it with an apology video."

> **4. Unethical brands exploit the customer's desire to self-actualize.**

What happens when a brand dangles self-actualization, but never follows through on fulfilling the promise? The consumer ends up hanging on, spending more, and waiting for what they were promised.

With unethical brands, "What happens on the way to the promise will ensure that you never self-actualize and therefore always need them. So you renew and you renew and you renew because the conclusion is 'it must be me doing something wrong.'"[6]

Identity Marketing invites consumers to become the best version of themselves. It's a powerful motivator that can be seriously effective.

Knowing what unethical brands do and being familiar with unethical marketing tactics can help you be a more conscious consumer. You can check your own practices to make sure you always implement your Identity Marketing strategies with integrity, honesty, and an ethical desire to connect your customer with what they truly want and need—versus what you want.

Another serious issue we see with Identity Marketing? Losing focus on who your marketing is about and who you're calling your consumer to be.

Identity Marketing, done well, builds a brand connected to your consumer's identity or aspirational identity.

Identity Marketing, done poorly, builds a brand centered on turning your consumer into a mini-version of you.

Remember the Enneagram coaching founder from the beginning of this chapter? They'd become an Enneagram coach themselves, so that's what they were selling to others. This was a big mistake to make with their audience, who were mostly interested in the personal insights and applications of the Enneagram, not in starting a new career as a coach.

Your goal isn't to invite your customers to become you, or make the most money possible off each customer.

The goal is to figure out who your customer is, and who they want to be. And to invite them to become the best version of themselves.

> ✓ **KEY TAKEAWAYS**

- Buyers are more discerning, less trusting, and more lost than ever.
- This is your chance to build a powerful identity affinity with your customers.
- Your brand's identity has to be about your customer—not you.
- An inauthentic identity never sells.

THE CURE FOR YOUR CONSUMER'S CRISIS

CHAPTER FOUR

A Better Way to Market and Sell

~~BUY THIS~~
BE THIS

If you opened my closet right now and sorted through the heaps of clothes in there, you would find a shocking amount of workout gear—leggings, shorts, yoga pants, moisture-wicking tops, workout tanks, and maybe even a $182 sports bra that's supposed to fix my posture.

I own far more fitness apparel than any normal person really needs. So why do I keep spending my hard-earned cash on more workout gear?

Because I see myself as a fit person.

If I'm being honest, my original desire to be fit was mostly born of vanity. I wanted to be in shape because I liked the way I looked. Like many of your consumers in a pre-2020 world, my identity was largely surface-level when it came to this category of self. I had the luxury of caring about my physical appearance above anything else.

Slipping into a pair of Lululemon leggings or a form-correcting sports bra made me feel like the person I want to be: healthy, vibrant, strong, capable. And swimming in enough disposable income that I can choose to spend hundreds of dollars on workout pants and bras. (If you're wondering where that all stems from, pop over to Chapter 5 and see why we have Barbie to thank for some of this!)

Then my entire world shattered when my little sister was diagnosed with an aggressive form of breast cancer in October 2023. And while my closet stayed stuffed with workout gear, the reason for wanting to hit the gym and my need for seventeen pairs of workout leggings changed dramatically.

Being by my sister's side as she faced down intense, brutal treatments that ravaged her body completely changed how I thought about working out and fitness. The appearance aspects were tossed to the side in favor of a deep longing to *live*, and for as long as possible.

I didn't want to look good in my jeans. I desperately wanted to live to be a hundred, staying active and strong enough to be here for my children and to enjoy our life together. The shift from vanity to longevity represents a significant, deepening change in my own self-concept and identity.

As I'm writing this book in 2024, my sister is thankfully cancer free and on her way to rebuilding her health and retaking charge of her life. But who I am and how I see myself has completely changed. And I'm not the only one.

Your customer is not the same person they were a few years ago. In fact, most consumers have formed an identity that goes deeper than surface-level desires in the face of all the world has thrown at us. We've collectively gone through traumas that have forced us to abandon frivolous wants.

Your buyers are less superficial and more discerning than they were, pre-pandemic. Every choice has more weight. Every buying decision carries a greater meaning.

Your buyers are deep, they are smart, and they are sophisticated. If you want your marketing to work, you absolutely must acknowledge that your ideal customer's identity has deepened and shifted.

Marketing still works. It just requires more

than scare tactics, appealing to vanity, or false urgency. Effective, ethical marketing taps into and reaffirms the honest, deep feelings your buyers have in a way that supports, encourages, helps, and inspires.

BUYING DECISIONS = HABITS

James Clear perfectly describes how our habits validate what we believe about ourselves in his book *Atomic Habits*,[7] that has sold over 20 million copies.

Recently, I was rereading Chapter 2, and I was struck by how 99 percent of marketers approach marketing *bassackwards*.

Clear focuses on habit formation, but his principles directly apply to buying decisions, too. Your purchases are your habits.

In *Atomic Habits*, Clear explores how most people try to form habits from the outside in. They look at the outcome they want, determine what process it will take to get there, and then they try to repeat that process to obtain the outcome they desire. And most new habit creation fails.

But his conclusion aligns with our belief about Identity Marketing: If you can align your habit

PROCESSES • OUTCOMES • IDENTITY

OUTCOME-BASED HABIT

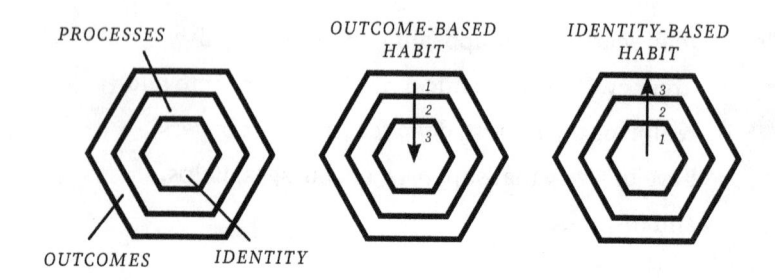

IDENTITY-BASED HABIT

with who you want to be, your aspirational identity, you can make your new, desired habits more consistent.

The connection between identity and consumer behavior works in two ways: Our identity directs our choices about what to buy *and* what we buy reinforces the way we perceive ourselves and our identity.

Clear understands identity to be a motivating force that drives consumer beliefs and behaviors.

So how do we take this habit-buying link and use it to inspire effective marketing plans?

Most marketers start with the desired outcome. What does our client want? What does our client need? What is our customer missing or struggling with?

You traditionally begin the process of marketing your goods and services by focusing on what your consumers will achieve by making their purchase.

But like we established in Chapters 2 and 3—this isn't working as effectively anymore.

Our customers don't believe us when we tell them we know what they need. They don't trust us to tell them how we can help. And this is why we have to do something different.

But if outcome-based marketing isn't the way, what's the alternative? How can we infuse our marketing with the knowledge and motivation Reed and Clear have outlined for us?

Identity Marketing flips the focus. Instead of starting out with what your customer wants to happen ... focus on who your customer wants to be. Their identity!

Clear explains:

Outcomes are what you get. Processes are what you do. Identity is what you believe.

> *"The word identity was originally derived from the Latin words 'essentials,' which means being, and 'identidem,' which means repeatedly. Your identity is literally your 'repeated beingness.'"*[8]

If we as marketers, sales people, business owners, and leaders don't shift how we see our role in a customer's life—not to sell them something but to help them become something—we'll miss out on the greatest opportunity we've ever been given, right at the perfect moment in history.

A consumer's behaviors are a reflection of who they are or who they wish to become. Our identity emerges out of our purchasing habits. What we buy, say yes to, and extend to others, is an embodiment of our identities.

The more we repeat the purchase or behavior, the more we reinforce the identity associated with our actions.

Building a brand that affirms your customer's belief that they are a person who oozes health, vitality, and financial security is a much more successful way to get someone to hand over their credit card than trying to convince them they want washboard abs.

Research supports the validity and impact of Identity Marketing.

Of 2,000 surveyed gym-goers, 69 percent said that having nice workout clothes made them feel good and motivated them to work out more frequently.[9]

We have all probably shared the experience of buying something because we liked what it said about who we are or how it led others to perceive us.

Every single company, serving every type of buyer, can use Identity Marketing to make a name for themselves and create a loyal, engaged audience.

No matter what you're selling or who you're selling it to, every human being, in every walk of life, in every economic situation is asking the same three questions:

- Who am I?
- Where did I come from?
- Where am I going?

And when your brand can provide an answer that resonates with your buyers and amplifies their aspirational conception of who they are and where they are going—you win. Every time.

> **✓ KEY TAKEAWAYS**

- Most marketers approach marketing the wrong way—focused on outcomes-based marketing strategies.
- The more effective marketing approach is identity-focused—answering your customer's question: "Who do I want to be?"
- Humans' identities emerge from their purchasing habits.
- Your marketing is more effective when you talk about what your customer can be instead of what they should buy.

PART TWO:

The Undeniable Power *of* Identity Marketing

CHAPTER FIVE

Resuscitating Brands and Companies

Featuring Mattel's Barbie

> Don't call it a comeback.
>
> —LL COOL J
> *Mama Said Knock You Out*

Actually ... that's exactly what it is.
So I guess you *can* call it a comeback.

RESUSCITATING BRANDS AND COMPANIES | 81

2023's blockbuster hit movie *Barbie* doesn't start with a little girl who loves playing with Barbies. Instead, when we first meet Sasha (the teenager who Barbie thinks needs her help), she's full of rage and criticism for who Barbie is and what she represents.

> "Come on Sasha."

> "Give it to her."

> *"Destroy Barbie."*

> "You've been making women feel bad about themselves since you were invented. You represent everything wrong with our culture. Sexualized capitalism. Unrealistic physical ideals. You set the feminist movement back fifty years. You destroy girls' innate sense of worth. And you are killing the planet with your glorification of rampant consumerism … You fascist."[10]

The brilliance of Sasha's diatribe is that it clearly lays out the stereotypes and criticism of Barbie in real life. She's sexualized capitalism, her proportions are unrealistic, and she makes girls feel worse about themselves.

And at her worst, that *is* Barbie's identity.

Or should I say *was?* Because Mattel and Barbie represent one of the greatest Identity Marketing comebacks in the history of capitalism and toys.

Barbie was born into a man's world, where everything, from the workplace to the toy industry, was dominated by men.

But as Liz Maglione, VP of global marketing communications at Mattel, said onstage at The Cult Gathering in 2023, "Through Barbie—girls could dream without limits."[11]

Named after inventor Ruth Handler's daughter Barbara, the doll anticipated the feminist wave of the 1960s and was built to give girls just as many opportunities and dreams as big as Ruth's son, Ken, had.

Mattel's Barbie was a massive hit. Barbie gave girls bigger futures and more options to dream of in the '60s, as she took on professional careers outside of being a teacher, nurse, or secretary.

Mattel welcomed the first Black Barbie in the '70s, broadening her representation and encouraging a more inclusive experience for *all* girls, and Barbie became a CEO (underrepresented, just like in the real world) in the '80s. She celebrated her fiftieth birthday milestone in 2009.

Barbie was a permanent fixture in most girls' toy boxes and playrooms, and she had grown up with the times, keeping pace with (or even anticipating) a brighter, more equal horizon for women.

And then in 2014, things changed.

Nathan Baynard, former VP of global brand marketing for Barbie, painted a clear, grim picture of Barbie's (and Mattel's) downfall in his talk with Liz Maglione at 2023's The Gathering:

> *"Barbie had lost her own narrative. Far from the layered it-girl that she had represented for years, moms started to view Barbie as one-dimensional. To anyone close to the business, it was subtle before it was obvious. We had been shy about innovating. The brand had been atypically quiet as culture, media, and new social pressures often worked against girls."*

Trail-blazing Barbie had failed to keep up with the real-life experience girls and women were facing, and the consumer backlash was intense.

Even as Dove, a major beauty company, saw their "Real Beauty" campaign going viral in 2014, gaining serious traction by promoting women's *real* bodies, in all shapes, sizes, and colors, celebrating the true diversity of women, Barbie was featured as a cover model for *Sports Illustrated's* swimsuit edition.[12]

Though the feature was well-intentioned, it highlighted the serious gap between the identity Mattel championed for Barbie and the *real* identities (and struggles, doubts, and fears) of the girls Barbie was designed for.

As Baynard succinctly put it:

> *In what was conceived as a strategically innovative and well-intentioned statement on empowerment, Barbie's singular take on beauty and perfection was way out of sync with culture.*
>
> *Mattel saw Barbie as she had always been, a model of aspiration, but moms, on the other hand, increasingly viewed the brand as vapid and worse, uninspiring, as their girls found it harder and harder to connect with Barbie as they always did.*
>
> *Girls wanted to see themselves in our dolls and we allowed Barbie to get complacent about the realities of a rapidly changing world. We had unintentionally failed girls, misunderstanding how valuable it was for every girl to see herself and her world reflected in our dolls.[13] In what was conceived as a strategically innovative and well-intentioned statement on empowerment, Barbie's singular take on beauty and perfection was way out of sync with culture.*

In 2014, Barbie sales hit their lowest point in fifty years, suffering double-digit declines. For most brands, this would be the beginning of the end. Barbie had lost the plot and Mattel was left marketing an identity that was neither aspirational nor desirable.

Barbie had failed girls.

But instead of giving up, accepting fate, and throwing in the towel, Mattel decided to realign Barbie's identity with what their consumers *actually* wanted for their own identities.

Barbie's identity realignment had the marketing team at Mattel drawing up a new strategy and eliminating redtape and barriers so they could actually transform their approach. The marketing leaders focused on putting the right talent in the right roles and creating a playbook to blaze a new path and keep everyone on track for a total Barbie transformation.

Mattel had created Barbie as the original girls' empowerment doll. In order to bring Barbie back to her original identity, they had to realign their marketing and messaging with what "empowerment" meant for girls in 2015. This realignment left the 1960s-identity of Barbie behind, so they could embrace a new identity that would resonate with modern girls (and their moms).

The result?

A "You Can Be Anything" campaign, that put young girls into specific adult jobs in the real world—soccer coach, veterinarian, college professor, traveling business person—and tied it all back to girls playing out those roles with their Barbies. It was no longer just Barbie who could be anything she wanted to be. The girls who played with Barbie were preparing to take on their own dream jobs and important roles.

This new campaign took Barbie "from fashion model, to role model."[14]

Mattel tapped into the real-world problems facing modern girls through their "Dream Gap" initiative. Maglione and Baynard said it was designed to address the gap, starting as early as age five, that exists between girls and their full potential. They created more than 175 looks for Barbie that included a wide range of skin tones, ethnicities, eye colors, hair textures, and (shockingly) body dimensions.

They leaned into social media and used Barbie's online platforms as a way to champion her new, modern identity, engaging with their audience and building a massive following of 3.5 million on Instagram and 2.1 million on TikTok.

THE $1.5 BILLION-DOLLAR PAYOFF

And then there was Barbie, 2023's summer blockbuster hit, directed by Greta Gerwig and starring Margot Robbie as Barbie and Ryan Gosling as Ken. Mattel took a serious risk giving Gerwig creative control over a move featuring their brand, and it paid off.

Women turned out in droves for the iconic film, which went on to be the highest-grossing movie of 2023, raking in $1.446 billion—the highest-grossing film ever released by Warner Brothers (the company responsible for all eight Harry Potter films) and the fourteenth highest-grossing film of all time.

The film also boosted sales for Mattel. The brand saw increased revenue, thanks to their realigned, identity-focused marketing strategy. Barbie products grossed $1.54 billion for Mattel in 2023.

One of the final scenes of the *Barbie* movie features the ghost of Ruth Handler, the inventor of Barbie, telling the doll: "I created you so you wouldn't have an ending."

And thanks to the brilliant Identity Marketing strategies at Mattel, Barbie will continue to delight another generation of girls, highlighting new paths and encouraging girls to dream even bigger to embrace their full potential.

IDENTITY IS YOUR BEST COMEBACK TOOL

What a comeback story: for the brand, for the company, and for Barbie herself. Mattel succeeded because they put Barbie's identity—grounded in modern girls' identities (and the identities their mothers want for them)—at the forefront of every marketing decision.

What worked for girls in the 1960s, and even the 1990s, no longer resonates with girls of the twenty-first century. The consumer's identity had outgrown the brand's identity, and if Mattel wanted to keep Barbie relevant and profitable, they had to tap into the modern identity of their target audience. Barbie's new identity helped girls embrace an empowered identity of themselves. That sells.

If you don't know who you are, your prospects won't either. And all the marketing strategies and brilliant ideas won't work if the identity you're marketing isn't both clearly defined and desirable.

Fifty years after her invention, Mattel had forgotten who Barbie was. That made it impossible to connect with and attract their target audience. Marketing leaders had to put in the time and energy to figure out who Barbie was before they could build out and execute a successful comeback campaign.

Does your brand need to orchestrate a comeback? First you need to take your business to identity therapy; to discover who you are, where you come from, and why you're here. Without that identity knowledge, you're at a distinct risk of alienating your ideal customer, and becoming painfully irrelevant to those you serve and sell to.

Imagine me, a Cuban-American toddler playing with my very White, very large-chested Barbie in the late 1980s.

I have a distinct memory of climbing down the stairs in my family's small townhouse to beg my mom for a double-dose of my Flintstones vitamins. When my mom asked me why I needed more vitamins, I confidently told her I needed them because "Yo quiero boobies, como los Barbies!"

I was a Latina three-year-old who desperately wanted boobs to match my stereotypical Barbie doll. Barbie's identity, so clearly ingrained it was evident to a toddler, was out of touch and problematic. It would be thirty years before social changes would demand a new, more approachable Barbie.

SO WHAT?

You don't need to lead an organization the size of Mattel to learn valuable lessons from Barbie's comeback.

We all started our businesses and careers for a reason. But so often, in the grind and hustle of doing, building, scaling, and climbing, we lose sight of the identities we started with.

We forget who we started out trying to serve. We lose the *why* behind our company, and stop focusing on the consumer's aspirations, being consumed instead by our own. That's exactly what happened to the Barbie team. And it's likely happening to each of us, on some level.

The invitation for a comeback is out there calling your name, inviting you to not only realign your brand's identity with your ideal customer, but to enjoy more revenue, more success, and more fulfillment as a result of your effort.

We'll get into the nuts and bolts of how to structure that comeback in Section 3. For now, let's focus on learning from Mattel's success and honestly considering whether it's time for our own comeback.

> ✓ **KEY TAKEAWAYS**

- When your brand's identity no longer aligns with your customer, sales will decline and you will lose market share.
- Mattel charted a great example of a comeback based on identity.
- If you don't know who you are as a brand and a business, your prospects won't either.
- You need to be able to clearly articulate who you are, where you're from, and why you're here if you want to remain relevant and successful.
- It's easy to lose our prospects' identities in our own hustle and ambition.

CHAPTER SIX

Tapping into Unprecedented Market Share

Featuring Taylor Swift, the NFL, Red Bull, and GoPro

> Teamwork makes the dream work ... and rakes in billions of extra dollars and millions of new fans.

When Travis Kelce was interviewed at the 2024 Cannes Lions—the Oscars of the advertising world—he was asked about how his podcast with his brother Jason, has grown:

> *"We were happy to have dog food sponsors in the beginning, and now we can kind of pick and choose who we want to represent the podcast."*[15]

What he's talking about? The real, tangible effect of one of the most massive brand collaborations we've ever seen. A collaboration that led to a hundred million-dollar offer from Wondery, Amazon's podcast branch, for the Kelce brothers' podcast, New Heights.

We're talking about the collaboration between Swifties and NFL fans.

It started with the relationship between Taylor Swift and the Kansas City Chiefs' tight end, Travis Kelce. But the collaboration far exceeds public interest in a romance.

To understand the power of this collaboration, we have to dig into the depth and power of the formidable community of Taylor Swift fans who call themselves Swifties. The term was coined by the fans and acknowledged by Swift in a 2012 interview, where she said:

> "My fans came up with a name for themselves and it's so cute! They call themselves Swifties and it's adorable, 'cause they made it up on their own."[16]

The Swifties don't take their self-appointed, star-approved identity lightly. In order to better understand the history and relevance of the Swifties, I sat down and chatted with Olivia Levin, a Swiftie and the longtime supporter behind @swiftieforeternity, one of the biggest Swift fan accounts on Instagram with over 600,000 followers.

When I asked Levin to define the difference between a casual fan and a Swiftie, she said:

> *"Swifties are the hardcore ones who are super, super invested in every aspect of Taylor and her music. So, the people who decode the Easter eggs, the people who listen to her music almost every day, or just have such a personal connection with the albums. It's not just like you're a fan of any other artists, and I think it's partially because of this parasocial relationship that's been going on for so long with her. She gets so raw and honest with music. So we do feel like we know her. We feel like we can relate to her stories and the things she's been through."*

Swifties feel personally and emotionally connected to Swift. They're as invested in the details of her life and the surprises she hides in songs, music videos, and outfits, as they are in her music. And these hardcore fans show up for their girl.

Swift recently broke Elvis Presley's record for most weeks spent at # 1 on the Billboard album chart as a solo artist, with sixty-eight weeks. Her worldwide Eras Tour has raked in over $1 billion and the economic impact she's made on the cities she visited came to an impressive $4.3 billion in the US. Swifties put their money (and they're spending a lot of money) wherever Swift is, and that now includes the NFL (National Football League).

As for NFL fans, they're notorious for their allegiance to their team. They can be found doing anything from wearing a hot, rubber dog mask for an entire game to represent the "Dawg Pound" for the Cleveland Browns, to drunkenly throwing themselves into the middle of tables at a parking lot tailgate as the Buffalo Bills, "Mafia" is fond of doing.

Grown men paint their faces, don their jerseys, and fully live out their passionate fan identity for three and a half hours on a Sunday afternoon while their team fights it out on the field.

The NFL has always been a dominant force in America, with an estimated 16.7 million viewers tuning in each week in 2023.[17]

So what happened when Swift showed up at a

Kansas City Chiefs game to support her boyfriend, Travis Kelce?

The Identity Marketing collaboration of the century.

Swifties followed their leader directly to the NFL, embracing football games, the Chiefs, and the ins and outs of the game with the same intensity they apply to Swift's music, personal life, and trail of infamous Easter eggs.

When I asked Levin about the impact she's seen since these two powerhouse stars collaborated, she said:

"It's absolutely insane to me, the impact that they've had on these two communities. Now you have fathers and daughters watching football. You have like these five-year-old girls watching football because they want to see Taylor and Taylor's boyfriend on the field."

With Taylor in attendance at games, female NFL viewership spiked 53 percent for teen girls, 24 percent for women 18-24, and 34 percent for women 35+ in 2023. Travis Kelce's jersey sales increased 400 percent.[18] And *New Heights*, the sports podcast Travis hosted with his brother Jason, got a huge boost in viewership.

The podcast saw a 4.5-times increase in weekly reach for listeners thirteen and older in the weeks following Taylor and Travis's romantic involvement, and their audience shifted from 32 percent female to 50 percent female.[19] This increase in viewers led directly to their nine-figure podcast deal with Amazon.

It's fascinating to note that even after the Swifties flocked to their show, Travis and Jason didn't stop talking about football. Their podcast is still mostly insider football talk and discussion about their respective teams. Swifties became fully-fledged 92-percenters, the identity-based nickname chosen by *New Heights* listeners.

We've also seen dads, boyfriends, and husbands, decked out in #87 jerseys, accompanying their daughters, girlfriends, and wives to the sold-out Eras Tour concerts across the world.

Cetaphil, a skincare company, ran an entire ad campaign in 2023, that showed dads across the country connecting with their daughters over football, now that Taylor Swift was part of the NFL conversation.

Local businesses have benefited from the collaboration, too. Olivia Levin told me about meeting a small business owner in Kansas City who had sold a Chiefs ring to Swift:

"I was talking to one of the owners, who said

her life has never been the same since Taylor wore that little ring from her store, because then they had thousands and thousands of orders and it kind of put the store on the map."

So whether the love story is one for the ages or not, the brand collaboration we've witnessed between Swifties and the NFL fans has generated billions of dollars in revenue, shot a podcast to the top of the charts, benefited small, local businesses, and forever linked two of America's most passionate identity-based fan groups.

The Swifties-NFL fan collaboration brought two separate, distinct consumer groups together for massive gain.

But what happens when companies that share an audience get together?

ADRENALINE JUNKIES UNITE

GoPro and Red Bull both appeal to an adrenaline-junkie, extreme sports demographic of young, active individuals.
While GoPro cameras capture thrilling moments of adventure and daring, Red Bull, a maker of energy drinks, has long sponsored these extreme events.

In 2012, before they were officially working together, Red Bull sponsored the Stratos project. This project featured Felix Baumgartner's record-breaking skydive from the edge of space. That feat was captured using GoPro cameras, providing breathtaking footage that was shared worldwide.

In 2016, Red Bull and GoPro decided to make their collaboration official. Red Bull gained equity in GoPro, while GoPro became the official provider of point-of-view imaging technology for all of Red Bull's events.

This collaboration started organically, with both companies recognizing the potential value of officially having a stake in the other's business.

According to Valens Research, GoPro's market share in the action camera market increased by 5 percent after the collaboration with Red Bull, and Red Bull reported a 7 percent increase in sales in regions where joint marketing campaigns with GoPro were executed.[20]

They've also found success with limited-edition co-branded products, like the GoPro HERO cameras with Red Bull branding, that have consistently sold out whenever offered.

WHAT CAN COLLABORATIONS DO FOR YOU?

Don't have a Swiftie-level fan base for your company? Don't worry! The good thing about collaborations is that they work on every level.

One of the major benefits of an identity marketing-fueled collaboration is amplified reach and exposure. By partnering with another brand, you get access to a new audience. That means you have new eyes on your business. New customers evaluate how you fit into or improve their identity, with the added benefit of the trust that comes from their allegiance to the brand you're collaborating with.

Collaborations also lead to increased brand loyalty and devotion. This is where identity really comes into play. If your new audience from the collaboration can infuse your brand into their identity, their loyalty will long outlast the duration of your collaboration.

Whether or not Travis Kelce and Taylor Swift's relationship stands the test of time, there will be women across the country who continue to watch NFL games and tune into the *New Heights* podcast because it has become part of who they are. (I say this with firsthand experience, as a now-dedicated *New Heights* fan, with Swift or without her.)

The opportunity for market share expansion that collaborations offer is next level. Red Bull was able to capture a significant percentage of the point-of-view technology market, without creating any new product or offer. This market share expansion is available to every business who finds a smart collaboration.

Collaboration also provides new revenue opportunities. You can generate entirely untouched streams of revenue when you partner with the right organization.

SO WHAT?

Let's take this out of the NFL/Swiftie stratosphere and look at how collaboration can work in real life.

Suppose you own a bakery located in a small shopping pavilion, and you decide you want to use the power of identity-based collaboration to improve your sales.

There's a hair salon next door. You've chatted with the owner, but you don't see how your baked goods could specifically appeal to the women who go into the neighboring salon.

What do croissants and balayage have to do with each other? Not much. But that's why we focus on the identity of the customer, not the outcomes or results of what we're marketing. Think about what your shared customer wants or needs.

Women who have to sit in a chair for two hours while their hair processes (yes, it really does take that long) want a little snack. Getting your hair done is a form of self-care, and indulging in a delightful Danish or cinnamon roll feels like the cherry on top of a relaxing appointment.

So you offer to sell fresh bakery items to your salon neighbor, who begins advertising hair appointments with a complimentary croissant or muffin and coffee.

Her bookings increase because this is secretly what every woman wishes was happening at her hair appointment. You make more sales to her as her appointments fill up. And now, there's a whole group of women who look forward to getting their hair done, because they also get a delicious treat they might not indulge in otherwise.

Together, you market the identity of a woman who cares for herself and deserves a little treat. Et voilà: the power of identity-based collaborations!

> **✓ KEY TAKEAWAYS**

- Collaborations can forge new customer identities or build on a shared customer identity
- Identity-focused collaborations provide amplified reach and exposure, increased brand loyalty or devotion, market share expansion, and new revenue opportunities
- The benefits of a strategic collaboration outlast the duration of the collaboration itself

CHAPTER SEVEN

Developing A Cultlike Following

Featuring the Dallas Cowboys Cheerleaders and Russell Brunson's 'Funnel Hackers'

> "People don't buy products, they buy identities. They want to be someone, and your product can help them become that person."
>
> —RUSSELL BRUNSON

Imagine you've had a dream to follow in your mom's footsteps since you were six years old. Your parents fully support your dream, and spend thousands of dollars sending you to specialist training and camps for your career passion.

You train and practice and spend your childhood and teenage years focused on your dream career.

Then the day comes. After grueling interviews and tryouts, you make it.

You achieve your lifelong dream job.

And it pays you less than $10,000 a year.

Wait. Who would possibly spend years and tens of thousands of dollars, to prepare for a job that pays so little?

The hundreds of women who audition to become Dallas Cowboys Cheerleaders each year.

The Dallas Cowboys Cheerleaders—collectively known as DCC—began in the 1960s.

The cheerleading squad was originally populated by high school cheerleaders, but in the 1970s they changed their look to the signature "hot pants" they still wear today and moved to employing adult women who were eighteen and older.

The DCC became an integral part of the Cowboys experience. "America's Team" isn't complete without the cheerleading squad, America's Sweethearts.

Hundreds of women audition each year for thirty-six spots. And once they make it, the job is grueling.

During the eighteen-week season, the women practice from 5 p.m. to 11 p.m. most evenings. Then there are the long game days on Sundays or Mondays, photo shoots, public appearances, cheer camps for kids, and daily workouts.

All of this for, (at the absolute maximum for a veteran who does most, if not all, of the public appearances) a salary of $75,000. Most DCC earn far less. Yet thousands of girls dream of, and hundreds of women audition for a chance to be DCC.

The status far outweighs the salary and demands in most of these women's eyes.

DCC is the pinnacle of cheerleading. Once you're part of the DCC family, that's a badge of honor you can proudly display for the rest of your life. Women happily take on second jobs and work 15-hour days to support their dream, because being DCC means more than sleep or money.

In the words of one DCC:

> *"You're becoming a whole different person when you put that uniform on."*[21]

HACKING YOUR IDENTITY

Step into a Funnel Hackers Live event for more than two minutes and you'll see just how devoted these online entrepreneurs are to their community and cause.

The Funnel Hackers movement was built by Russell Brunson, the co-founder of ClickFunnels—a software platform that allows business owners to create sales funnels.

Brunson built ClickFunnels without any venture-capital funds, and within five years, the platform reached $100 million in revenue and over 55,000 software users.

Funnel Hackers didn't accidentally grow into a cultlike movement or community. Brunson planned it that way.

While building his business, he (somewhat controversially) shared that he studied historical figures who successfully built a loyal following—including Jesus and Adolf Hitler.

He hadn't set out to build a business. Brunson intentionally created a passionate following known as Funnel Hackers.

Within the niche group of hyped-up business owners who use ClickFunnels to (hopefully) make their millions is a group of business owners who have already made millions: The Two Comma Club. To qualify, a business must create a ClickFunnel that generates at least one-million dollars in gross revenue and verify your sales through a rigorous verification process.

Members in this exclusive group get to strut across stage at a Funnel Hacking Live event, shake Brunson's hand, and proudly display the framed golden vinyl symbol of their achievement. Two Comma Club members have *made* it, their million-dollar revenue achievement proudly on display for all to see.

Being able to designate yourself as a Two Comma Club member is often incentive enough for other businesses to want to work with you. The designation is so highly regarded in certain circles that business owners will spend two million in order to make the one million in their funnel and be included.

Two Comma Club members see the money they spend to get into the club as an investment in their identity.

They want the recognition, status, and membership in the club more than they want the money it costs to get there.

Whether it's online marketers craving a Two Comma Club membership, or women dedicating their lives to become DCC, the cult-like identity is worth every drop of sweat and dollar from their bank account for true devotees.

WHY IS CULTLIKE DEVOTION SO POWERFUL?

Intense devotion to an identity isn't random. When you use Identity Marketing to create a cultlike following, you are essentially fulfilling the top three levels of Maslow's hierarchy of needs.

114 | IDENTITY MARKETING

In this motivational theory proposed by American psychologist, Abraham Maslow, human needs are broken into five categories that build on one another to form a pyramid. The most important needs are at the bottom, and as one ascends the hierarchy of needs, the less essential to life the needs become.[22]

Belonging to a group fulfills the love and belonging tier of needs, but when you can create a cult-like attraction so your audience equates their identity and aspirational self with being part of your group, you can ascend even further up the

SELF-ACTUALIZATION
The peak of existence, when you become your best self.

ESTEEM
What you need to feel good about yourself, like respect, self-esteem, freedom, and status.

LOVE AND BELONGING
What you need to feel connected, like friends, family, and intimacy.

SAFETY NEEDS
What you need to feel secure, like a job, health, and resources.

PHYSIOLOGICAL NEEDS
What you need to stay alive, like air, food, shelter, and water.

Here you can see how the hierarchy of needs stack up from most essential to life to least.

pyramid—getting into esteem and the coveted tier of self-actualization.

When you fulfill someone's core needs and provide them a sense of self-actualization, there's nowhere else for them to go. You create the ultimate identity that not only feels good, it literally fulfills all of your customer's needs.

The power of promised status is one of the strongest seductions in the world.

The potential fulfillment and self-actualization is so desirable that devotees will spend serious time, money, and energy to attain that status.

And once they obtain it? It's an indelible part of their identity. Once a DCC, always a DCC. And same goes for Two Comma Club members. They never let go of that status once it's achieved.

SO WHAT?

We can't hide from the obvious ethical dilemma that is intertwined with creating a cultlike devotion to your brand.

As a leader and marketer, I don't recommend studying or following problematic figures or creating unethical payment, rewards, or results for your devotees.

The stories of DCC and Funnel Hackers are undeniably powerful examples of how strong a desired identity can be, and to what levels a desirable identity can push people.

But that doesn't mean you have to take advantage of that power. Try replacing a status-based identity with a values-based identity.

Cultlike devotion is often seen at a smaller level, so this is a perfect way for small- and medium-sized businesses to tap into the power of Identity Marketing.

I've seen a coffee shop become a cult-favorite in a small town because they invited customers to become part of a mini-community: offering board games, hosting themed events, and offering really comfortable seating to encourage long stays. The values-based identity of "community" resonated with patrons of all ages who will choose to visit this coffee shop with mediocre coffee over local shops with better espresso.

Alex Cattoni, the founder of the Copy Posse (the New School for Copywriters), created a positive cultlike following by building a community based on powerful non-negotiables. The Copy Posse gives up-and-coming copywriters an alternative to the "bro marketing" (an in-your-face, aggressive style of marketing commonly used by younger male entrepreneurs) copywriting education that dominates the scene and invites members to join the Posse in their mission to "de-douchify the internet."[23] A mission defined by more authentic, less pushy marketing that centers around words that ignite community, change, conversation, and credibility.

When you know who you are and invite your customers to adopt a values-based identity that resonates with them, you can use the power of Identity Marketing to create a cult-like following of your own.

AUTHENTICITY

We're fiercely real and loud as hell.

We believe in loudly standing up for what we believe in – even if it means ruffling a few feathers. While we're sweet, we'll never sugarcoat it. We strive to always be straight up, true to self, and fiercely real, which means owning our flaws and listening to feedback.

INNOVATION

We blaze the trail with courage and compassion.

The Posse is a global army of rad humans who want to make an impact in the world with disruptive, bold and people-first marketing. We're here to shake things up, dream big and break a few rules along the way. Sorry, not sorry.

Non-negotiable examples reproduced with permission from copyposse.com/about

✓ KEY TAKEAWAYS

- When the potential identity is desirable enough, people will spend more money trying to become the identity than the identity will actually help them make
- Cultlike devotion includes unavoidable ethical questions and dilemmas
- A values-based cultlike identity is better than a status-based identity

CHAPTER EIGHT

Disrupting Saturated Markets with Cause

Featuring SMASHD's Nicole the Intern, and Presidents Trump and Reagan

> It's time to uncover your hidden army of evangelists ... *even if you think they're not there.*

What do you do when you've got an underdog brand of non-alcoholic drinks that no one can pronounce and barely anyone knows about, but you're determined to break into one of the most saturated industries in the world?

DISRUPTING SATURATED MARKETS... | *121*

You get the internet to rally around an intern "trying to prove her boss wrong."

Before we get into the impressive details of one company's social media campaign to simultaneously create a cause and a new brand, let's set the stage.

An intern at Mixoloshe (pronounced like a take on mixology, not "mix-a-loash" like many of their customers thought) created an Instagram account called @thebestmarketingstrategyever on April 13, 2024.

The intern, fondly known as Nicole the Intern, posted her first video to the account. In it, she's smashing a can of Mixoloshe with a baseball bat with a simple statement superimposed over the video:

"60 days remaining to prove to my boss that smashing this can is more effective than his entire marketing strategy"

In the caption of the post, she wrote:

> **thebestmarketingstrategyever** If I don't hit 500k followers by 6/10 I'm fired 🫠

In a single Instagram post, Nicole the Intern created a cause millennials and Gen Z could get on board with: Sticking it to the boss.

This wasn't about selling drinks, it was about rallying around an "underpaid intern" who had something to prove. Instagram wanted to be part of the force that took Mike the Boss down.

Nine days in, Nicole reported that they had doubled their website traffic since she started smashing cans. As her audience grew, so did the stakes.

Her boss, Mike, continued to offer more rewards for hitting her goal of 500k followers—not only would she not be fired, but she would get a promotion. Then he offered to let her rename the company.

This is when things got seriously interesting.

The comments on Nicole the Intern's videos blew up, with user-generated content pouring in, of followers smashing cans. Thousands of people chimed in to say they had purchased or were invested in the cause.

Fifteen days into her challenge, Nicole the Intern gave the cause a name, dubbing her followers the "Smash Army."

> **rantatoulliee** this is it. this is the one that made me join this valiant cause.
>
> 15w 379 likes Reply

> **pharr_away** Rooting for you, Nicole! 500k seemed like a stretch at first but we're all so invested now. I had no awareness or interest in this product and I've since checked it out on Amazon because of you. You're killing it 🌑!!
>
> 14w 70 likes Reply

She had played around with different props and costumes, but the army helmet and "army" approach really struck a chord with her audience, so she ran with it.

With a name to unite them, the Smash Army continued to gain steam and show up for the cause, while Mike the Boss refused to learn their name or give the Smash Army any respect, referring to them as the "Smash Squad" or "Smash military group." The disrespect only fueled the Smash Army to crush their goal.

> **sflhousehermit** Who's here just because they want someone's boss to be wrong
>
> 13w 78,067 likes Reply

Gary Vee, serial entrepreneur and four-time *The New York Times* best-selling author, caught wind of the Smash Army and joined the cause, even stepping into a video toward the end of the challenge to smash a can himself and salute Nicole in her iconic army helmet.

With sixteen days to go until the deadline, Nicole the Intern hit her goal of 500,000 followers on Instagram. She had successfully created massive support for a simple, but relatable cause: proving the boss wrong.

Smashing cans was fun, but it was the collective energy and effort channeled toward taking down authority and getting a win for "the little guy" that gave the Smash Army the will and power to grow as it did.

The ultimate results of Nicole's "Best Marketing Strategy Ever" campaign speak for themselves:

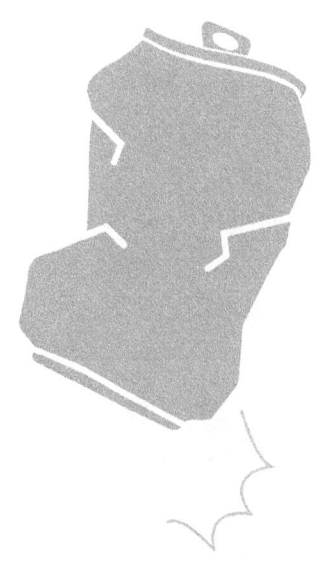

THE RESULTS

$0 spent on ads—the entire campaign was organic

$35,000 spent on creating videos

0 → 527,000 followers in just sixty days

250 million impressions and 150 million plays on Instagram

500,000 website visits

60,000 email sign-ups

9x increase in sales

> Identity Marketing gives you the power to promote your
> Comments → Content

PROMOTING COMMENTS TO CONTENT

The smartest thing Nicole the Intern did was pay attention to her comments.

She looked at what people were saying, what they were asking for, and what they were inspired by, and she promoted those comments to her content. The best causes have a clear leader and still respond to and engage with their followers.

Nicole the Intern set herself up as a young woman set on proving her boss wrong, invited over 500,000 people to join her cause and used their words, passion, requests, and interest to fuel her campaign.

This campaign was never about buying drinks. Nicole the Intern never asked her followers to buy *anything*. Instead, she invited them to become part of a greater cause and join the Smash Army.

By leveraging Identity Marketing, this company took an underdog brand that no one could pronounce and claimed a bold stake for themselves in the super-saturated beverage market.

ONE CAMPAIGN SLOGAN, TWO DIFFERENT IDENTITIES

In a less wholesome and more polarizing fashion, President Trump also created a cause voters could get behind. In the run- up to the 2016 election, his campaign slogan "Make America Great Again" (MAGA) had taken on a life of its own.

This is not a political argument or endorsement. We just can't pass up the opportunity to examine the identity marketing at work in Trump's MAGA campaign. Because, agree or disagree with his politics, the campaign was powerful and effective enough to win a national election *twice*.

Instead of asking voters to choose him in November, (the voting equivalent of "buy this"), Trump invited voters to become more American.

It wasn't even an original idea, but his commitment to the identity marketing aspect of the slogan turned it into a massive, driving force.

Ronald Reagan was actually the first to use a version of the slogan in a presidential campaign. When he ran in 1984, Reagan's slogan was "Let's Make America Great Again." Same words, but a very different energy and ethos.

Reagan carried 44 of 50 states in one of the largest landslide elections in US history, [25] using "Let's Make America Great Again" as a unifying call to action. He invited every American to be part of the "great" America he envisioned, and they responded.

In 2016, Trump took the phrase and created a very different cause. His America was divided, and only the *most* patriotic were invited to join him. The key here is that patriotism was defined as aligning with Trump's policies and ideology.

The mere suggestion that America needed to be made great *again* implied that what was happening now was not working. It called back to unspecified glory days of power, privilege, and prosperity, and invited voters to join the "winning" team.

Trump saw the stark divide between political parties, and instead of trying to unify the two sides like Reagan had, he chose to drive the divide deeper. Issuing a clear ultimatum: you're either a patriot who wants to win with us or a loser who doesn't want what's best for this country.

By tapping into the identity of voters and making the choice as stark and divisive as possible, Trump built a rallying cause behind the idea of MAGA. Voters didn't want to be seen as weak or a member of the "establishment."

Despite his absolutely unrelatable lifestyle and economic status, Trump was able to make himself one of "the people" by emphasizing his anti-establishment position. He encouraged voters not to trust the government while simultaneously asking them to put him in charge of the government.

As incongruous as those invitations read on paper, in practice, people were relieved to finally hear someone give a public voice to all the distrust and criticism they had privately thought for years.

Politics are deeply personal. Trump capitalized on his ability to create a cause—Make America Great Again—that aligned with a large percentage of voters' internal doubts, beliefs, and identities.

Donald Trump and Ronald Reagan each ran campaigns based on essentially identical identities with a similar slogan, but each offered a completely different invitation and championed diametrically opposed intentions.

One used "Make America Great Again" to unify the people, the other used it to divide. They both saw success in their own time.

Following his 2016 run, Trump attempted to use the slogan with a slight variation "Keep America Great" to carry his 2020 campaign, only to lose to Democratic nominee, former Vice President Joe Biden. The message just wasn't the same.

When he returned for yet another campaign in 2024, Trump brought "Make America Great Again" *back*, only this time it was open for customization. The adaptation of the slogan into "Make America Healthy Again" and the MAHA movement[26] gained serious traction and helped lead Trump's path to victory.

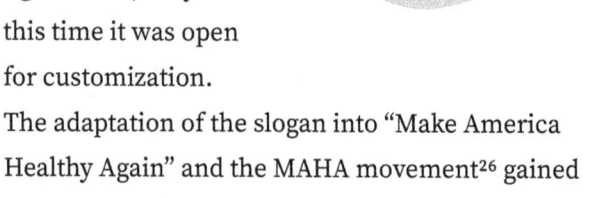

Each time the words "Make America Great Again" were used, they had a different context. The strength of the story *behind* the words influenced the strength of the slogan and the entire campaign. (We'll learn how to create meaningful context behind your own words and identity when we get to the Identity Code in Chapters 10 – 14.)

CREATING AN IDENTITY-BASED CAUSE LEADS TO MAJOR DISRUPTION

An intern generated 500k+ followers, growing sales ninefold, and rebranding a (now) multimillion-dollar company in just sixty days. Both an actor and a reality TV star became the president of the United States of America.

Disruption at its finest on two very different stages, and in wildly differing markets.

Any time you're trying to disrupt an industry or promote your business in a field with a high barrier to entry, you've got to do something serious to stand out. Creating and marketing an identity-based cause is one of the most effective ways to disrupt a saturated market, get serious visibility, and achieve unexpected results.

Creating a cause sets you apart as a category of one in a densely populated, pre-established place. This gives you the appearance of novelty and the ability to invite customers to become part of something that's both bigger than themselves and also promotes who they want to be.

What cause can you invite your customers to be part of?

- **Environmental:** Cleaning up a neighborhood, building global sustainability practices, or reusing and recycling

- **Social:** Charity and fundraising, community development, or diversity and inclusion

- **Health and Wellness:** Public health campaigns, personal fitness, improving wellbeing, or research

- **Educational Causes:** Scholarships, literacy programs, or skill development

- **Humanitarian Causes:** One-time disaster relief, refugee support, or supporting impoverished or high-need populations

- **Animal Welfare:** Wildlife protection, cleaning up outdoor spaces, or animal rescue

- **Arts and Culture:** Donating to local artists or productions, preserving historical sites or monuments, or supporting fundraising

- **Politics and Advocacy:** Voter registration, social justice, or donations to a specific cause

- **Technology and Innovation:** Digital literacy, crowd-sourced solutions, user-generated ideas for improvement

- **Corporate Social Responsibility:** Employee volunteering programs, ethical sourcing, fair trade

The key to a successfully disruptive cause is linking the cause directly to how your audience sees themselves or who they want to be. Identity Marketing is so powerful because it ignites an intrinsic need or desire within your customer base that encourages action and rewards participation.

Inviting your customers to become part of a cause can be an overarching marketing strategy or a one-time or limited-time promotion. You can build an entire brand around your cause or use it to generate additional revenue or build interest for a specific time.

Asking your customers to align themselves with your cause is a different strategy than asking customers to join your community. A community (like we explored in Chapter 7) revolves around like-minded individuals sharing similar interests and communicating about what they have in common. A cause requires sustained energy and support, focusing more on affecting change than creating connections.

Both can be effective ways for Identity Marketing to play out, you just need to be clear on what *your* audience is looking for and how you want to leverage your brand's Identity Marketing.

SO WHAT?

If you're trying to break into a saturated marketplace, you need a reliable disruption strategy.

Creating an identity-based cause your customers can rally around and get behind is one of the fastest, most effective ways to break down barriers to entry and get more visibility.

Cause-based identity marketing doesn't require a large budget. We saw Nicole the Intern generate serious website traffic, email sign ups, and sales with no ad spend and a starting budget of $0 (that eventually grew to $35,000 as she proved her campaign) spent on creating her Smash Army videos and campaigns.

You can do the same with even less if you're willing to leverage social media and user-generated content.

Some brands lend themselves to a related

cause more naturally than others, but every single brand can find a cause that can unite their customers and gain serious traction. If you choose to use Identity Marketing to help you disrupt your industry, make sure the cause is directly linked to who your audience is or how they want to see themselves.

A cause on its own isn't that appealing, but an identity-based cause is irresistible.

✓ KEY TAKEAWAYS

- Identity Marketing gives you the power to recognize the identity your customers are interested in assuming (more about the concept of learning to promote your comments to your content in Section 3) and connect with your audience on a whole different level
- If you want to disrupt a saturated industry, inviting your customers to join an identity-based cause is the best way to stake your claim
- You can invite your customers to join a cause as a long-term strategy or a one-time/limited-time promotion

CHAPTER NINE

Transforming Intangibles into Ridiculously Profitable Tangibles

Featuring Nike, Red Ants Pants, and The Pink Bee

> "A shoe is just a shoe until somebody steps into it."
>
> —SONNY VACCARRO

The movie *Air* tells the origin story of Nike's Air Jordans, one of the most iconic shoe brands that has ever existed, created in partnership with the GOAT himself, Michael Jordan.

In the film, the Nike board is pitching Jordan

to become their basketball star and the namesake of their basketball shoe line. Matt Damon, who plays Sonny Vaccaro, famed sports marketing exec., delivers this chilling line in an impromptu speech to Jordan and his team at the pitch meeting:

> *"A shoe is just a shoe until somebody steps into it. Then it has meaning. The rest of us just want a chance to touch that greatness. We need you in these shoes, not so you have meaning in your life, but so that we have meaning in ours."*[27]

It's a powerful line in the film, and according to Vaccaro himself, close to the actual conversation he had with Jordan.[28] And it worked. Jordan chose to partner with Nike in 1984 for an unprecedented 2.5 million-dollar deal (that would be roughly 6 million dollars in 2024) and an agreement that he would receive a cut of the profits. *Forever.*

When he inked this deal, Michael Jordan effectively turned his intangible identity into one of the most tangible, profitable products of all time.

While his basketball career was undeniably a success—he played fifteen seasons and won six NBA championships with the Chicago Bulls, and earned two gold medals with the US Olympic team—it inevitably came to an end.

But Air Jordans, a product inspired by his athleticism and identity as a rebel, are still selling like absolute wildfire, thirty years later.

The success of the shoes and Jordan's identity are inextricably linked. One wouldn't exist without the other.

LEANING INTO THE DISRUPTION IDENTITY CREATES

Air Jordan 1s were designed to be more bold than typical basketball shoes of the time, with their signature red and black splashed all over the high-top silhouette. They also included innovative air cushioning that responded to Jordan's innovative playing style and overpowering athleticism.

The color and design of the shoe led to it being banned by the NBA shortly after its release in 1984, after Jordan wore the sneakers in an exhibition game against the New York Knicks. It violated the NBA's uniform guidelines, which indicated that shoes must include a significant amount of white.

Instead of redesigning or pulling the Air Jordan 1s, Nike leaned into Jordan's rebellious, win-at-any-cost image and ran ads to capitalize on the controversy and pay for his fines. The campaign resonated deeply with the public, who idolized Jordan and led to Air Jordans exceeding their initial sales goal of $3 million. Instead, Nike raked in $126 million in their first year of sales.

Identity Marketing is the secret to turning intangibles into unbelievably profitable, tangible goods. Getting to own and wear a piece of Michael Jordan's identity was more lucrative than anyone had even dared to dream.

Air Jordans started as basketball shoes, but quickly became a cultural icon that defied boundaries and were embraced by athletes, celebrities, musicians, fashion icons, and 12-year-old kids on the playground.

The success Nike saw with commercializing Michael Jordan's career and identity led to unprecedented product success and set the benchmark for future endorsements. The shoe line continues to innovate and set the standard for sneakers, generating billions of dollars a year in sales and enjoying an iconic status.

Identity is unequivocally marketable and tangible.

AN IDENTITY AS STRONG AS ITS CUSTOMERS

The founder of Red Ants Pants, Sarah Calhoun, grew up doing challenging physical labor and relying on men's clothing that didn't fit her body or support her needs because no workwear options existed for women.

There's an entire segment of the female population that is hard-working, industrious, and in need of clothing that fits their bodies *and* their jobs. Sarah saw women like her being ignored and overlooked, so in 2006, she decided to do something about it.

Red Ants Pants was named to reflect the identity of her customers—in red ant communities, the

The success Nike saw with commercializing Michael Jordan's career and identity led to unprecedented product success and set the benchmark for future endorsements. The shoe line continues to innovate and set the standard for sneakers, generating billions of dollars a year in sales and enjoying an iconic status.

Identity is unequivocally marketable and tangible.

AN IDENTITY AS STRONG AS ITS CUSTOMERS

The founder of Red Ants Pants, Sarah Calhoun, grew up doing challenging physical labor and relying on men's clothing that didn't fit her body or support her needs because no workwear options existed for women.

There's an entire segment of the female population that is hard-working, industrious, and in need of clothing that fits their bodies *and* their jobs. Sarah saw women like her being ignored and overlooked, so in 2006, she decided to do something about it.

Red Ants Pants was named to reflect the identity of her customers—in red ant communities, the dan's innovative playing style and overpowering athleticism.

The color and design of the shoe led to it being banned by the NBA shortly after its release in 1984, after Jordan wore the sneakers in an exhibition game against the New York Knicks. It violated the NBA's uniform guidelines, which indicated that shoes must include a significant amount of white.

Instead of redesigning or pulling the Air Jordan 1s, Nike leaned into Jordan's rebellious, win-at-any-cost image and ran ads to capitalize on the controversy and pay for his fines. The campaign resonated deeply with the public, who idolized Jordan and led to Air Jordans exceeding their initial sales goal of $3 million. Instead, Nike raked in $126 million in their first year of sales.

Identity Marketing is the secret to turning intangibles into unbelievably profitable, tangible goods. Getting to own and wear a piece of Michael Jordan's identity was more lucrative than anyone had even dared to dream.

Air Jordans started as basketball shoes, but quickly became a cultural icon that defied boundaries and were embraced by athletes, celebrities, musicians, fashion icons, and 12-year-old kids on the playground.

female ants do most of the heavy lifting and manual labor. Calhoun wanted her clothing to be a real-life embodiment of the women she worked with and admired.

The women who purchase Red Ants Pants workwear and live out the ideals reflected by the clothing gather in a virtual community dubbed the "Anthill colony." The community is connected by a Red Ants Pants-powered blog called *ANTecdote*,[29] where they can read stories about other women in the Anthill, get the latest news, and stay in touch.

One of the best features of the clothing is the Red Ant Challenge. The seamstress who makes each piece of workwear embroiders a red ant into a different location. When women who wear Red Ants Pants meet each other, they're invited to compare the locations of their red ants. If two women share a red ant in the same spot, they can take a photo and send it in to the company to each receive a free t-shirt.[30]

The Anthill, the ANTecdote blog, and the Red Ant Challenge are all key elements in promoting the shared identity of the women who make up the customer base. They see themselves as part of a community—a member of the Anthill—and not just a woman working in manual labor or on a farm alone.

Calhoun was able to turn the identity of the hard-working, industrious woman into a community and a tangible product, helping women in male-dominated industries feel more connected, supported, and celebrated.

Giving customers something they can hold, use, or wear that feels intimately connected to *who they want to be* is a powerful marketing tool.

SO WHAT?

Inviting your customers to align with your brand's identity is one thing, but giving your customers a physical, tangible opportunity to *be* part of your brand is the next level of marketing.

But if you don't have a product-based business, it may feel impossible to make your identity tangible.

While yes, product-based businesses have a more direct line to tangibility, service-based businesses can also tap into the power of transforming the untouchable into a highly desirable, attainable, tangible object.

Megan Sumrell, a time management and productivity expert and owner of The Pink Bee, gets a lot of hate about the name of her business.

When choosing the name for her work-life harmony business, she landed on a name that was highly personal and held significant meaning to her. But she was told by mentors and peers that it was a terrible name: "It doesn't tell anyone what you do."

But you would be shocked what the name does for her brand.

In a conversation with Sumrell, she said that she regularly gets DMs, texts, emails, and physical mail from clients and fans of her brand when they find pink bees out in the wild. Hundreds of people have shared pink bees they find with messages like, "This made me think of you and your business!"

The Pink Bee has become part of her clients' identities. They call themselves the "Queen Bees" and lean into all things bee- and pink-related. For clients of Sumrell, pink bees are a reflection of their desire to be organized, productive, and excellent at time management.

Her service-based business has even found its way into tangible products like an app and a planner, all centered around what she teaches her clients and what it means to be a "Pink Bee."

Giving your customers a tangible piece of the identity you've built is the best way to lock-in those lifelong loyal, engaged fans we're focused on creating.

When you've created a brand that people want to wear, tattoo on themselves, or even be buried in (shout out to Harley Davidson back in Chapter 1!), you've made it.

Now it's time to dive into Part 3 and learn how to take everything we've learned about Identity Marketing and actually do it!

You've got the knowledge, inspiration, and examples. Now it's time to put everything to work in your business so you can start creating legions of loyal customers, no matter *what* you sell.

> ✓ **KEY TAKEAWAYS**

- Identity Marketing can turn the intangible into ridiculously profitable tangible goods, products, and representations of your brand
- Tangibility is all about giving your customers a way to own, wear, or use the identity you've called them to embody
- Making your brand's identity tangible is the key to locking in your audience and generating lifelong customers

We'll see you in the next section for all the how-to tactics and strategies you've been waiting for!

PART THREE:

How to Create Lifelong, Loyal Fans and a Legendary Brand

(No Matter What You Sell or the Size of Your Budget)

CHAPTER TEN

The Identity Code

How to use an easy 4-step framework to unlock a marketable identity

The Identity Code™ is a proven framework that will help you install Identity Marketing effectively, whether you're a ten-figure corporation or an intern with no marketing budget (yet!).

This framework applies to everyone, from small and medium businesses to large corporations, solopreneurs, marketing teams of one, and sales professionals.

In the introduction of this book, we asked if you identify as a marketer.

If you do, you're already on track. And if you don't, by the end of these four chapters, you'll have so much how-to knowledge and confidence that you will want to identify as a *Marketer*.

We also got serious about the very real, unavoidable consumer crisis that is actively taking place. Your customer struggles to know *who* they are anymore. There's a huge pool of customers just begging to be seen and affirmed for who they wish to become.

If you can answer that call with a compelling, aspirational answer, you've just won yourself a whole slew of loyal buyers for life.

This section is *the* solution to the consumer's identity crisis and the dwindling efficacy of marketing and sales. This is the part of the book where you finally unlock the answer and create the solution that your customers are searching for.

In the following pages, you're going to:
- FIND your marketable identity
- PROVE that this identity resonates with your audience and is not only clever, but intrinsically connected to your customers' identities
- NAME your identity with a powerful origin story and context behind it
- DRESS your identity in a way that defines, humanizes, and elevates it

BUDGET FOR FAILURE

One of the reasons this proven process delivers serious results is because we create intentional space for failure. You'll learn more about how this works in Chapter 12 (the Prove It step), but for now it's important to know that you will experience failure in this process.

Not only is that okay, it's planned for and expected.

Hypothesis-style marketing includes test after test after test. The problem with testing, before the Identity Code™, was that it required a lot of money. Testing in the marketplace is a big expense. (But don't worry, there's a way to test that's not just affordable … it's free!)

When we budget for failure, we go into our marketing with the acceptance that nothing is ever an instant hit. We don't need immediate perfection, but we do need results. This is why we test, rework, test, refine, and test again.

Only once we have a proven concept that our audience has *already* adopted, will we put money behind a campaign, branding, and website updates.

Whether you're a budget-strapped solopreneur, or a CEO with a strict CFO (Chief Financial Officer) on your case—this is good news.

Here's the truth: You may not have the stardom of Taylor Swift, the budget of Barbie, or the 120+ year history of Harley Davidson ... *yet*.

But guess what?

You don't need any of that to start.

The Identity Code contained and explained in the next four chapters is the secret to unlocking legions of your version of Swifties, bringing in major revenue like Barbie, and establishing the loyalty of Harley riders without any of the budget or fame.

TIME TO GET TO WORK

We're done learning about Identity Marketing. Now it's time to *do* Identity Marketing.

In the next four chapters, you have exclusive access to the proven Identity Code framework. It will walk you through the steps you need to take (in the order you need to take them) to discover and implement a marketable identity that can change everything.

Work through these chapters one at a time, making time to do the work within each chapter before jumping to the next. This process is structured the way it is for a reason.

Knowing and understanding Identity Marketing is helpful, but IMPLEMENTING Identity Marketing in your business is transformational. All you have to do is follow the steps, put in the work, and then reap the rewards.

Prepare to be legendary!

Additional resources can be found at ***identitymarketingbook.com.***

CHAPTER ELEVEN

Find It

How to secret shop yourself without spending millions

If you're an existing brand with an established audience, chances are your people have already come up with an identity for themselves. This makes your job so much easier, because the work is done for you. Now you just need to find that identity. (If you're not an existing brand or you're just getting started, keep reading. There are specific ways you can still apply this first step fruitfully.)

The creation and evolution of identities within brands is complex and typically organic. This process happens within brands, often without anyone noticing until the identity has become an established, accepted part of business. There are psychological reasons for this—humans have an inherent need for social belonging. We tend to label ourselves in ways that affirm our positive beliefs about ourselves, and we love cognitive consistency, which is why we make choices that align with the labels we've adopted.[31]

In Chapter 6, we discussed the powerful collaboration between the Swifties and the NFL. Taylor Swift, (even being the marketing mastermind that she is), didn't create the term. Fans dubbed themselves "Swifties" in the late 2000s, as her popularity grew with the release of her *Fearless* and *Speak Now* albums.

And if you can remember all the way back to Chapter 1, we examined the lifelong commitment of Harley Davidson fans who build their identity around riding "hogs." That moniker actually started back in the 1920s, when a group of Harley racers known as the "Wrecking Crew" would celebrate their wins by taking their mascot, a pig, on victory laps.[32]

The term "hog" organically became associated with Harley Davidson bikes and riders. Because it resonated with their riders and was such a known reference, the company created the Harley Owners' Group (H.O.G.) in 1983 and cemented the user-generated term eighty years after the company first started. But it started with riders and fans of the bikes.

When I interviewed Kierra Conover, former marketing manager at Gap, on my podcast, she cautioned brands to always "look inward before outward,"[33] and we're going to echo that advice here.

How can you find the identity you can market to resuscitate a dying brand, tap into unprecedented market share, develop a cultlike following, disrupt a saturated market, or transform the intangible into ridiculously profitable tangibles?

It's actually pretty simple.

You need to secret shop yourself.

BECOMING AN IDENTITY SECRET SHOPPER

Secret shopping is a 2 billion-dollar global industry, with 80 percent of US companies using the service at some point. This is a strategy that *works*. Companies like Apple, Shell, and McDonalds use secret shoppers, and we see practically every industry, from retail to financial and automotive services, benefiting from secret shopping services.

With traditional secret shopping, someone comes to your business without your knowledge and evaluates:

- Quality control
- Employee performance
- Customer experience
- Competitive advantage

The goals of using a secret shopper are typically to improve the customer experience, increase sales, and encourage better employee performance.

Identity secret shopping works a little differently. Instead of evaluating your business's performance, you want to step in and evaluate your customers, to find the identity they associate with your brand. Then you can amplify and intentionally market that identity.

The beauty of identity secret shopping is that the answers are already there waiting for you, as long as you know where to look and what questions to ask.

This is where we put into practice the idea of promoting your comments to content, just like Nicole the Intern did so well. She didn't start out calling her followers the Smash Army. Instead, she tried many different approaches to see what theme and content resonated most.

When the army schtick got a big response from her growing follower base, she paid attention to her comments and saw the militant response and commitment to the cause growing. Her comments shouted "We're on your team, we're fighting with you!" and she listened. It's no coincidence the Smash Army loved being called the Smash Army. Nicole secret shopped her brand and promoted what she found waiting for her in the comments.

Where can you look to secret shop your brand?

Social Media Platforms

Check the comments, hashtags, and mentions about your brand on platforms like Instagram, Twitter, TikTok, and Facebook. What words, terms, or titles are your fans using when they reference your brand or the use of it?

Even if everyone isn't using the same term, you may be able to pick one that you feel encompasses what you want to promote about your brand and amplify it yourself.

Community Forums and Groups

Look at discussions in dedicated forums, Reddit threads, Facebook Groups, or other online communities where fans gather. These spaces are often where organic identities form and gain traction.

You'll get the most authentic ideas and results when you shop around what's being said organically. Put people in a market research room or send them an official survey and they'll automatically be more guarded and corporate and less likely to share the identity gems you're searching for.

Customer Reviews and Testimonials

Analyze reviews on sites like Amazon, Yelp, Google, or your website. Customers might use certain terms or names to refer to themselves collectively.

Looking through your reviews is one of the best ways to identify specific marketing language to use outside of an identity moniker. These are gold!

Brand Hashtags and User-Generated Content

Pay attention to hashtags that reference your brand outside of direct tags or the exact business name. Users may be creating content using specific names or phrases to self-identify as part of your community without you even knowing it.

Merchandise, GIFs, and Fan Creations

Does your brand generate fan-made merchandise, art, or other creations? These non-licensed creative efforts often reflect the names or terms your community uses to describe themselves.

Pay attention to parodies and jokes made about your business, too. Sometimes a little self-deprecation can lead to a powerful identity that is ultimately beneficial.

Fans of the 2009 hit TV show *Glee* owned their identity of being dorky musical theater kids or fans and co-opted what could have been seen as a negative into their proud title of Gleeks—a portmanteau of *Glee* and geeks.[34]

Event Attendee Feedback

Whenever you host a virtual or in-person event, gather feedback from attendees. Pay attention to how they describe the community and who they connected with or learned from.
During virtual events, look for clues in the chat to see what people are saying during sessions and in casual conversation. At live events, make it a point to walk around and listen. See what's resonating with people. We talked to one business owner who was considering investing in an existing event. He attended the live event to see how participants

responded to the brand, and met one woman who had left a session and come back with the logo of the event tattooed on her arm. He knew right then there was a meaningful identity at play among the audience.

Influencer and Ambassador Programs

What language do your influencers, ambassadors, or affiliates use?

These are great insights into how people outside, but closely related to, your brand perceive their related identity. Influencers tend to be more conversational and less constrained in their communication, which can lead to the rich, descriptive language you're looking for.

Sales Call Transcripts

Pull up past sales calls and look for common words, terms, or phrases your potential customers are using when discussing your offer. What questions are people asking? What are they most interested in learning? These questions, as well as the specific verbiage used, are excellent places to find potential identities that resonate with your buyers.

Secret Shopping sounds great and all, but what if I'm a new business, or I don't like the identity I find?

Great question! While some brand identities are created by your customers, you still have the power to promote or disregard specific terms, names, and identities. Even fan-created terms like Swiftie and Hog are only given permanence by the brand itself embracing and promoting the term. So if you don't like the identity you're finding (or there's no identity for you to uncover yet), you can still control the narrative.

Follow in Russell Brunson's footsteps (jump back to Chapter 7 if you need a refresher) and create an identity on purpose from ground zero. We'll talk about this in more detail in the next chapter.

You can also secret shop your competitors! Most of the people in your industry are sleeping on Identity Marketing, so they're not using any of the marketing gold available in their social media, reviews, community groups, and all over their public communication.

IDENTITY CREATION GONE WRONG

The marketing world is littered with failed attempts to sell a brand-generated identity to an existing audience. Regardless of how clever you are or how deeply you research, an identity *must* be adopted and embraced by your audience or it won't ever work.

Let's learn from the failures of others so we don't repeat their mistakes.

The "Pepsi Generation"

Back in the 1980s, Pepsi tried to create a cool, youthful identity to compete with Coca-Cola's nostalgia and classic Americana appeal, but it never really stuck. The whole idea felt forced and lacked genuine cultural relevance—*why* should young people think of themselves as the Pepsi generation? The brand couldn't give them a good enough reason, and they ultimately abandoned the campaign and moved on to other strategies.

Microsoft's "Scroogled"

From 2012-2014, Microsoft attempted to steal market share from Google by creating a collective identity for everyone who was skeptical of Google's data collection practices. They referred to it as people who didn't want to get "Scroogled," but the term was a huge flop and no one really adopted the identity.

This approach failed because it was too negative and was focused on attacking the competitor more than it was focused on building a positive identity or community for Microsoft users.

Budweiser's "Bro Code"

Basing your marketing campaign on fraternity culture is typically a big no. Budweiser found this out the hard way in 2009 when they attempted to create a sub-identity for their drinkers, uniting them around the loyalty and camaraderie of the "bro code."

Needless to say, this failed, thanks to its heavily sexist overtones and exclusionary, outdated ideas. Budweiser's audience was not into the negative stereotypes it emphasized about young men, and the company quickly stopped trying to make the bro code happen.

There are hundreds of more brand-generated, failed identities out there. This is why we recommend secret shopping your audience and discovering what they're telling you, instead of trying to spring a brand-created identity on them.

If you are going to generate and promote your own identity for your customers, you must have a deep understanding of your audience's genuine feelings, values, and desires before taking an idea to the identity drawing board.

Brand-generated identities fail when there is a disconnect between what the brand wants and how the customers see themselves.

As we see in the examples above, here's what you want to avoid when creating an identity for your audience:

- **Inauthenticity:** Every time an identity is forced, it fails. Customers can sniff out inauthentic branding from 100 miles away, and they will reject it every time.

- **Negative framing:** Sure, people like to complain, but they don't want to identify as a negative person. Negatively framed identities tend to backfire or be too divisive to unite a whole community.

- **Cultural irrelevance:** No one wants to adopt an identity that feels out of touch or outdated. Pay attention to the current cultural trends and opinions, making sure to "read the room" before marketing an identity to your people.

- **Being too corporate:** If an identity was created and approved in a boardroom, there's a good chance it's too corporate to resonate with real people. You want to get as close to a naturally occurring identity as possible, which means anything that's overly polished, clean, or corporate won't resonate with your customers.

SECRET SHOPPING YOUR IDENTITY

Congratulations! You've done the hard work of finding the identity your customers are asking for you to promote, so now it's time to validate that identity and make sure it will stick. On to Chapter 12!

FIND IT | *167*

CHAPTER TWELVE

Prove It

How to get immediate buy-in without outdated focus groups

Comedian Nikki Glaser stepped up to the mic at the Tom Brady roast and absolutely *crushed* it. She struck the perfect chord of mean, snarky, honest, and funny. Even host Kevin Hart was blown away by her performance, telling the crowd after she finished her set: "That's the beauty of roasting. There's an art to it, and when you get it right, g**damn, it's amazing."[35]

When you see a comedian performing in a Netflix special or onstage at one of the biggest roasts of all time, there's a tried-and-true process that has taken place off stage, usually in front of tiny crowds at dirty little comedy clubs.

That process? Validation.

Comedians don't just write jokes and then perform them in front of thousands. They get an idea and test it out with their friends and trusted fellow comedians. They take feedback and refine. Then they test the refined jokes in dusty basements and dark little holes-in-the-wall to see how the audience responds.

For her Tom Brady roast set, Glaser took the preparation and validation stage seriously. She was able to test out certain jokes with a live audience and decided what to keep and what to cut based on their reactions. She consulted with other professionals around where to draw the line with particularly sensitive topics like Brady's children.[36]

And all that practice and validation paid off.

When it comes to testing the identity you've found or want your audience to align with, take a page from the great comedian's book and validate, validate, validate. This will give you the power to create an accurate, appealing identity from scratch, even if you don't have an existing audience or you don't like the identity you uncovered from your customers.

This process involves meticulously testing every detail of your proposed identity to ensure it resonates with a wide audience. You'll feel confident and excited to market this identity once you *know* it will resonate.

MESSAGING IS YOUR MARKETING OUTFIT

In marketing, your messaging is like an outfit. Some outfits fit well while others just never quite work. Some messaging will go over fine, and some will go viral, like JLo's iconic, jungle-print Versace dress at the 2000 Grammys.

The key is not to get overly attached to one messaging outfit over another. You never know *what* will work! Sometimes your favorite "off the rack" marketing messages will turn out to be donations down the road, and that's okay.

Bottom line: If you don't at least try on the messaging, you haven't done the real work.

If you're reading that and thinking, *Great! That sounds like spending thousands on focus groups ...* I've got good news for you. Focus groups are not required for this activity. We don't want to trust focus groups too much anyway. Just look at Google's AI commercial that launched during the 2024 Olympics.[37] It passed through focus groups and then failed miserably live.

In an official statement released after the ad aired, a spokesperson for Google said: "While the ad tested well before airing, given the feedback, we have decided to phase the ad out of our Olympics rotation."

We're going to skip the focus group and try on our marketing messaging in front of people who can actually tell us if it's an iconic look or a major flop: our commenters.

PROMOTING COMMENTS TO CONTENT

We introduced the concept of promoting comments to your content in Chapter 11, and here we're going to expand on this idea and really put it into practice.

We'll revisit our favorite intern, Nicole, and her Smash Army to make this concept more concrete.

Nicole started off by trying different outfits and approaches in her videos. She donned colorful, furry onesies, hit cans with baseball bats, and wore a cowboy hat and cowboy boots before ever appearing in her (now iconic) army helmet.

In the first post featuring the intern in the army helmet, we see comments like:

> *"I've probably seen at least two other videos of hers and didn't follow. But this one, this one made me follow."*

> *"Best one so far fr [for real]."*

> *"One of my favorites thus far."*

> *"The salute got me."*

Commenters were really into the army vibe, and Nicole paid attention. She first showed up in the helmet ten days into the challenge, came back in the next post with it again, and then used a *Monty Python and the Holy Grail* clip to amplify the "intern vs. boss" narrative.

Her messaging shifted to promote what followers were sharing in the comments, and five days after the helmet was first introduced—Nicole the Intern called the group the "Smash Army" for the first time. This was a move from previous descriptions like "Nicole the Intern fans," grounded in the army motif that was really resonating.

Her audience went wild for the identity, embracing it and quickly referring to themselves as the Smash Army.

Nicole tested lots of different ideas, saw one that gained particular traction, and tested it further with a unifying title. If no one had claimed their affinity to the Smash Army, it might have remained a random hashtag that she didn't use again. But instead of falling into obscurity, it took hold. The Smash Army grew from 125,000 to 500,000+ in just a few weeks.

This is the general process we are going to refine, label, and replicate with your brand.

THE VALIDATION PROCESS

Follow this 4-phase process to successfully promote your comments to your content and test whether the brand identity you want to market has traction with your audience.

PHASE ONE:

Analyze the Sentiment and Meaning Behind the Identity

===

We start by evaluating potential content. Just because our audience calls themselves something doesn't mean we automatically use it. It's your brand, so let's make sure you protect what matters.

- **Look for comments that reflect a strong, positive association with your brand.** If a bunch of commenters dislike something about your brand, even if that's repeated, it's not a sentiment you want to amplify. You want to find things that resonate with the broader community and describe an identity you're proud to promote.

- **Check for engagement.** If a comment sparks a lot of likes, shares, or replies, that's a good sign that the sentiment resonates with your larger audience.

- **Be flexible.** Identify positive comments that are widely shared that may not perfectly match your desired identity. If the community loves it, shares it, and it reflects well on your brand, you may need to give up a little of your pre-conceived identity.

PHASE TWO:

Promote Comments to Testable Content

This step can require courage and a willingness to fail. Testing implies that it may not land with our audience, and that's okay. Nikki Glaser didn't crush her Tom Brady roast without putting a few terrible jokes out there with her test audience and accepting the negative response as a need to change.

To best gauge adoption of the identity within a short time frame, you should focus on high-impact, fast-response methods. These include:

- **Immediate engagement on social media:** Post content specifically referring to the identity term you want to use, for example: "Calling all members of the #vhive!" and track the number of comments, likes, and shares compared to your average post. A spike in engagement indicates positive reception of the term.

- **Instagram stories or polls on X or LinkedIn:** Ask your audience directly if they identify with the identity term you're considering. Posting a poll or story like "Do you feel like you're part of the V-hive?" gives you immediate feedback on who resonates with the term.

- **Direct Calls to Action:** Prompt your followers to use the identity name in their posts, comments, or tags with something like "Use #vhive in a story today and I'll reshare my favorites!" Then track how many fans take action.

- **Hashtag growth:** Note the usage of your identity-related hashtag before you start using it. Encourage your audience to use it over the week of testing. If you see a rapid or significant increase in usage, that's a sure sign the identity is being adopted by your customers.

- **Communication with active followers:** Identify the customers who interact with your brand the most through comments and DMs. Ask them what they think of the identity name you've chosen. See if they feel like it represents them. The reactions of this core group of engaged followers should be indicative of your broader audience.

- **Short-term campaigns:** Run a short challenge or contest using the identity name. Encourage followers to take action with the title, like "Post your favorite moment as part of the #vhive and win a $25 gift card!" The level of participation can be an indicator of how well the name is catching on.

- **User-generated content:** Encourage your audience to create content using the identity name and feature it on your account. Track the number of people who participate and pay attention to how they use the identity.

These strategies will give you a sense of overall adoption and connection to the identity name in as little as a week. Remember to judge the performance of the name against your typical social media engagement and interactions. It's not the overall number of likes, shares, and comments you want to track—it's how those compare to the rest of the content you normally share.

PHASE THREE:

Test Warm and Cold Audiences Separately

This is one of the most important steps, and one that most people tend to skip. People who know you, follow you, and engage with you are biased toward you. They'll have more tolerance for inaccuracies or vagueness than a random, cold person will.

Even the most seasoned marketers have made the mistake of applying warm audience results to a cold audience, and suffered the consequences. A cold audience doesn't know who you are or care about your brand—their level of understanding is significantly different from a warm audience's care and engagement.

You want to find an identity that engages both warm and cold audiences, so you will need to run cheap, cold ads that exclude your followers, website traffic, and email lists. This will get an accurate representation of how everyone will respond to your tested messaging.

PHASE FOUR:
Refine and Repeat

===

This is where you have to toughen up and be willing to take the feedback you've requested. Channel your inner Nikki Glaser and be open to making adjustments and changes based on what your audience tells you.

- **Track metrics** like engagement rates, shares, and comments to determine what resonates and what doesn't. Be cautious about talking yourself out of believing what the data is telling you—numbers don't lie.

    If a quote from a comment that you reposted on your Instagram leads to higher engagement than usual, consider exploring similar themes or language in future posts or turning the comment-inspired post into a broader campaign.

- **Iterate and expand.** Use the feedback you get to refine your content strategy. Continue promoting comments to content, testing different angles, and expanding on the ideas that resonate most with your audience.

- **Follow your audience's lead.** Pay attention to the feedback you receive on the comments you turned into content. These comments can clarify how your audience feels about the identity you're testing with them.

Validating your messaging helps you reduce the risk of failure. It gives you data-driven confidence and excitement, and creates an optimized entry to the market. This is the key to sustained success, and an identity that deeply resonates with your audience.

Now that you've found your identity and validated it, it's time to make your messaging irresistible. I'll teach you exactly how to elevate your brand's identity in the next chapter, so let's get to it!

CHAPTER THIRTEEN

Name It

How to give your identity a deep meaning without surface-level gimmicks

> "What's in a name?"
>
> —WILLIAM SHAKESPEARE

Shakespeare asked the same question in *Romeo and Juliet* that we're asking now. It's as timeless as it is important.

In Steps 1 and 2, you found your identity and proved that it resonated with your audience. You know who your customers want to be. Now it's time to give that identity a name.

This step isn't about choosing a catchy name or assigning a random one. It's about crafting a specific story; context behind the name of the identity we're preparing to market.

Our framework is designed to make the identity we're elevating feel human. Identity Marketing is personal. It's about connecting with the very real desires of the humans who trust us, like us, and buy what we're selling.

Naming this identity is akin to naming a baby. The name you choose carries weight, meaning, hopes, dreams, and intentions.

When choosing your baby's name, you don't just think about what's trendy right now or what you like. You imagine kids yelling their name on the playground. (Is there any way this could lead to unfortunate nicknames or embarrassment?) You project an image of the type of adult you hope your baby will grow up to be and assess whether the name will fit them then. (Will people take them seriously with this name at thirty-five?) You imagine cradling this sweet baby in your arms and whispering their name as they fall asleep. (Does this name encompass the love, hopes, and dreams you have for this tiny new person?)

The same thoughtfulness and intention is required when naming your marketing identity. This name is going to be adopted by your customers, used by thousands of people, and shared with outsiders. The name needs to carry the weight of your values, unique selling proposition, and quality of your products or services. It also reflects the way your customers see themselves and identify with your business.

Words matter. Studies have shown that your name causes a different reaction in your brain than any other name in your native language.[38] We love our names because they are the summation of who we are, what we stand for, what we've accomplished, and what we dream about. (This is why marketers use your name when they want you to pay attention to an email.)

THE ECONOMIC IMPACT OF A NAME

Behavioral science teaches us about self-concept—the mental picture of how we picture ourselves. Our self-concept is a combination of who we really are and who we want to be.

Behavioral science expert and co-founder and chief creative officer of HBT Marketing, Nancy

Harhut clearly explains the connection between our self-concept and our purchasing decisions in her 2019 keynote address *How to Hack the Brains of Donors, Members, and Other Humans*.

As Harhut explains, we buy things that communicate who we are to the world, relying on the implication of certain brands and logos (the "name") as an external reflection of our internal self.

We also see the economic impact of naming when it comes to being part of a group.

"Behavioral scientists have found that when people are labeled as part of a group, they quickly start to behave like the members of that group—even if they hadn't previously thought of themselves as part of that group!"[39]

The power of a name.

With brands, logos, and group labels, it's important to note that the power only exists when the name is desirable or aspirational.

The context *behind* a name and the identity summed up *by* a name is what gives a name power.

Before we get into the process of naming your identity, make sure you're asking, "Why *this* name?" Take all the purpose, context, and implications attached to the name into consideration as we move forward.

THE STORY MATTERS

Back in Chapter 8, we learned how Donald Trump's MAGA campaign was first used by Ronald Reagan in the 1980s, although with a dramatically different origin, meaning, and impact.

The similarities between the two figures can't be denied. Two men with entertainment experience—an actor and a reality TV star—running for the same office with the same campaign slogan. But with two very different meanings.

For Reagan, "Let's Make America Great Again" was a unifying call to put aside our differences and pull together as a country. To work together toward a better quality of life and prosperity. And he won 44 of 50 states in a historic landslide victory with the spirit and purpose behind that campaign slogan.

In comparison, Trump used the same slogan with a small revision, "Make America Great Again," and with a completely different ethos. Instead of a unifying message, MAGA was an ultimatum. You're either with us or against us, and if you're against us, you're wrong. Trump's campaign slogan was divisive, intent on identifying "real" Americans as those who followed his party line. And the slogan, again, led to victory.

"Make America Great Again" has been both a positive call to unity and a divisive call to separation. Same words, with wildly different impacts and meaning, thanks to the context and story that propels them.

LET'S GIVE YOUR IDENTITY A NAME

Now that we understand the power of a name and the importance of the context, story, and meaning *behind* that name—it's time to name your identity baby.

Remember, we're not pulling a random name out of the air. We're building an identity and a legacy that this name will encompass and stand for. And don't worry, I've got a process for you to follow.

The Birth Story

Where did your identity get its start? How was it brought into the world? People need to hear the origin story to truly connect with the identity you're inviting them to embody.

Yes, you're reading a book and following a framework to bring this identity to life, but the birth story of your identity goes deeper than this book or these steps.

If you found your identity through the method outlined in Step 1, you can tell the story of how your community created this identity and emphasize that it's a name given by the people, for the people. Give credit to your community and write your identity's birth story from a collective perspective. Refine what you share and be intentional about the way you craft this story, but it should feel like a collective effort.

If you proved that the identity resonates and aligns with your audience in Step 2, you can now tell the story of why you chose the identity and how it reflects your personal approach and perspective as well as the experiences and identities of your customers.

When discussing how the Smash Army came to be, Nicole the Intern said:

"In many ways, it might be me projecting my own identity onto them."[40]

She had come from a pageant world of perfection and beauty, where every image she shared had to be curated and look just right. Becoming

> **WE'RE THE NEW SCHOOL OF COPYWRITERS**
>
> The Copy Posse was started with one sole mission: **to redefine what it means to be a copywriter, marketer and entrepreneur today.**

Birth story example reproduced with permission from copyposse.com/about

the leader of the Smash Army, an identity grounded in carefree fun and the enjoyment of life, was a chance to let her fun side shine. She extended her audience an invitation to join this movement that was rooted in the carefree attitude she wanted to reclaim for herself, asking them to become part of the birth story narrative.

The birth story can be told from a first-person perspective, but should still directly connect to your customers and make them feel included.

Copywriter and marketer Alex Cattoni has a fabulous example of a birth story on her website. Turned off and offended by a lot of the manipulative, hypey, overly masculine marketing tactics she saw running rampant in the copywriting industry, she decided she needed to do something about it and took a stand for something different.[41]

This led to her creating the Copy Posse—an identity that started with the founder and grew to be embraced, beloved, and adopted by a whole new school of copywriters.

When writing your identity's birth story, it should include your:

- Mission
- Vision
- Core values
- Shared goals
- Where the identity started (from you or from your community)
- Who it includes

The identity's birth story should be an actual narrative, written to tell the story of how the identity came to be, what it stands for, and why it matters. This story should have a dedicated page where it lives on your website. It can also be included in your brand messaging guide or other marketing resources your organization uses.

Non-negotiables

Great marketing attracts the right people and repels the wrong people. You can't have massive attraction without repulsion—it's a good thing.

Identity Marketing is the perfect way to attract and repel. When you can align your brand's name with strong non-negotiables, you'll effortlessly separate your people from outsiders who do not connect with the identity you're marketing.

It's important to note that these are not exclusively your personal non-negotiables. This identity is the embodiment of your community's non-negotiables, the beliefs adopted and championed by the greater whole.

Alex Cattoni's Copy Posse, which we examined above, is a perfect example of how non-negotiables are incorporated into an identity's name. The Copy Posse is empathetic, fun, authentic, innovative, and full of integrity. They break the rules, make mistakes, and are serious about making an impact. Anyone who doesn't live their life—and run their business—with those priorities is not in the Copy Posse.

Inclusive Slogan

Consumers love a good slogan.

It's a simple, powerful way to tell people what your identity is all about. It's like a code that the people on the inside understand and can relate to, that makes them feel like they are part of a movement or an important community.

Teach for America, an organization that trains young leaders to step into some of the toughest classrooms across the country and improve outcomes for students in underserved schools, rallies both exhausted new teachers and experienced alumni around the slogan "One day."

It comes from their longer vision statement that reads, "One day, all children in this nation will have the opportunity to attain an excellent education."[42]

TFA members use the phrase "one day" to reference the importance of their work, the gravity of the problem they are working to solve, and almost as a password that encompasses the long nights, hard days, and dedication of the unique experience shared among members.

Your slogan should speak to the purpose, values, and non-negotiables of your identity without overcomplicating things or trying to tell the whole story in one short phrase.

Examples of identity slogans include:

"Just do it."

This recognizable phrase from Nike embodies the athlete identity Nike stands for—bold, fearless, ready to take action.

"A diamond is forever"

DeBeers coined this slogan in 1947 and it has remained a core reason why most couples choose a diamond as the gem for their engagement ring. This slogan made diamonds and true love synonymous and inextricably linked.

"Real Beauty"

We discussed Dove's Real Beauty campaign in Part 2, and this slogan is a perfect example of summing up the core of the identity you're marketing in a simple, easy-to-understand and relate to way.

"Easy, Breezy, Beautiful"

Did you finish that statement with … "Cover Girl"? This relatable, affordable makeup brand tells women exactly who they are for (and who they are not for) with this catchy slogan.

"Live to Ride, Ride to Live"

We can't leave Harley Davidson out of this conversation. Their slogan embodies the rebellious, freedom seekers who own their Hogs (and are buried in their branded caskets).

The Identity Path

When you invite your customers to become someone new, it's important that the path you're inviting them to walk down is clearly defined and highly desirable.

While it may seem obvious, you need to make sure the name you choose reflects the path your customer will travel.

We don't want to invite our people to simply be a different or heightened version of themselves. We're creating an all-encompassing, comprehensive identity shift that will transform them into someone new. It needs to feel dramatic.

In the example of the Copy Posse, Cattoni invited her clients to follow her distinct path to go from *copywriter* to *Posse member*.

In my business (which we'll discuss in more detail in Part 4), I invited members to go from *marketer* to *Rainmaker*. A Rainmaker is a sought-after marketing leader who achieves a level of mastery that transcends titles and status. Rainmakers possess the skills and mindset to break the cycle of burnout and self-promotion into roles of significant impact, with a career that resonates beyond the boardroom.

Taylor Swift lovers go from *fan* to *Swiftie*.

It's the next level. It's elite. It's a clear delineation between your customer and everyone else.

Write down your identity path and make sure you clearly welcome your customers to go from who they are now to the more desirable, more aligned identity you're inviting them to be.

USING THE IDENTITY YOU NAMED

Once you've gone through this process in order from start to finish, you're ready to put the name you've given your identity to work.

While it's tempting to skip straight to this step and just start using an identity name you like, if you don't complete the proper steps it will lack the gravitas, meaning, and purpose of an effective identity. There is a method to this madness.

You've done the work, you've built the name, and you've created the context. Now it's time to use it!

> *We'll use the fictional identity of "The Click Clique" (presumably for PPC--pay per click--marketers) as an example to show you how to use your own identity in your marketing and copy.*

Your identity name can be used in things like (but not limited to):

- **Website Copy:** Incorporate "The Click Clique" into your website's headlines, taglines, and Call-to-Action (CTA) buttons. For example, change a generic CTA like "Join Us" to "Join the Clique."

- **Social Media Bios:** Update your social media bios to mention the "Click Clique," e.g., "Leading the #ClickClique to new heights!"

- **Email Marketing:** Start your emails with a greeting that acknowledges the "Click Clique" such as "Hey Clique!" or "Dear Click Cliquers."

- **Blog Headlines:** Rewrite existing headlines to include or reference the "Clique." For instance, "The Clique's Guide to [Topic]" instead of just "Guide to [Topic]."

- **Ad Copy:** Update any running ad campaigns to include the term "Click Clique," ensuring that the identity is front and center.

- **Hashtags:** Promote a unified hashtag like #clickclique across all your social media posts. Encourage your community to use it whenever they post about your brand. Create additional, context-specific hashtags like #cliqueTips or #ClickCliqueLife to categorize content.

- **Stories and Testimonials:** Regularly feature stories, testimonials, and content from your "Click Clique" members. This not only builds community but also makes others want to be part of it. Highlight different members of the "Clique" each week on your social media or in your newsletters.

- **Content Series:** Launch a content series on social media or in emails that are centered around the "Click Clique." This could include interviews with community members, discussions on shared values, or deep dives into the brand's mission. Share behind-the-scenes content that makes "ClickClique" members feel like insiders, with exclusive looks at upcoming projects or decision-making processes.

- **Sales Scripts for Live Chat or Sales Calls:** Train your sales team to refer to customers as part of the "Click Clique" during interactions. For example: "As a member of the Click Clique, you'll love this product because …" During live chat or calls, offer exclusive deals by saying, "Since you're part of our Clique, I can offer you a special discount today."

- **Referral Program Copy:**
  - *Invite a Friend:* "Love being part of the Click Clique? Share the magic with your friends and earn rewards when they join the Clique too!"
  - *Referral Reward:* "For every friend you refer to the Click Clique, you'll both receive $10 off your next purchase. It's our

way of saying thank you for adding to our Clique!"

Your identity has a name. It's a real, living entity! The only thing left to do is give your named identity the elevated status and irresistible outfit it deserves.

Come along now. We're dressing up in Chapter 14, and this is the most fun step!

CHAPTER FOURTEEN

Dress It

How to make your identity feel real

One of the most powerful marketing moves you can make is to turn your intangible offer or service into something that feels tangible. This is great news if you're in e-commerce or a consumer goods business—you're solid.

But if you're in an industry like:

- Services (healthcare, finance, coaching, etc.)
- Online education
- Tech (SaaS (Software as a Service), software, etc.)
- Education
- Hospitality and Tourism

What are you supposed to do?

This is where we tap into the power of personification.

Personification humanizes your brand, product, or service. It gives your brand a personality and makes it possible to create emotional connections. The emotional connections generate joy, trust, and comfort.

When you successfully personify the identity you're marketing, you will differentiate yourself from your competitors and clearly stand out in a crowded market. It's easier to separate your brand from everyone else when you have a recognizable personality that's attractive to your customers.

Think about it like being at an office party where everyone is just talking shop talk and being their boring, buttoned-up selves. Then someone fun waltzes in with a cocktail, telling funny stories and making you laugh. Who are you going to remember at the end of that soirée? Not the generic, corporate clones.

WHY DOES TANGIBILITY MATTER?

Personification is an effective way to make an intangible brand more tangible, but why do we care about tangibility in the first place?

Being able to touch, feel, and interact with the things we buy impacts our behavior. Engaging multiple senses—sight, touch, sometimes even smell and sound—creates a connection between the customer and the product, engaging a psychological sense of ownership and increasing the confidence the customer has in the quality and efficacy of the product.

If you're marketing a service or digital product, you're clearly not able to tap into the physical benefits of tangibility. But there is an emotional aspect of tangibility that a personified brand can achieve without creating a physical good.

If you can trigger memories, a sense of nostalgia, or a strong emotional response—even with an intangible brand or offer—you can benefit from the emotional resonance of tangibility. This can be achieved through a brand that feels knowable, even if there's nothing to physically perceive.

Marketers of intangible goods can also access the benefits of customization and personalization. A highly personified brand allows a potential customer to feel like the brand—and its offers or services—were created for them. When a brand feels like a natural extension of the customer themselves, they feel a strong affinity and attraction to it.

Tangibility satisfies a human need for trust, emotional connection, and personalization, making products more valuable and desirable. Marketers who deal in intangible goods can use the power of a strategically personified identity to make the intangible *tangible* and enjoy the economic benefits.

WORDS FIRST

We went in a specific order with the steps to crafting the identity for a reason.

You can't touch the visuals—your logo, color palette, typography, and all the things that make your brand identity—until we've finalized the words *behind* them. Words persuade, while images make us feel. You need both to engage your buyers and make a sale, but the words (your persuasive argument) should guide the images (the vibe you want to create) so they can bring your words to life.

In my experience, when you get the order wrong and put visuals before the words, you end up with a beautiful brand that goes belly-up within eighteen months.

Words carry significant weight. They convey detailed information and give context to abstract concepts, feelings, and thoughts, allowing for nuanced communication and understanding. While images evoke an emotional response, words connect with humans on a deeper level, through storytelling and shared experiences. The emotional connection of words is enhanced when the specific words chosen align with the beliefs and values of the listener (your customer).

An image can't make a persuasive argument, but your words can. Words are the very foundation of the practice of persuasion. It is with our words that we share opinions, reason, and present a cohesive, compelling argument.

Images are excellent for drawing attention and provoking a quick, instinctive response, while words are the context and meaning that give your customer a reason to keep paying attention, dig deeper, learn more, and finally, take action.

PERSONIFIED BRANDS

We're all caught up on the power of personification, the importance of tangibility, and the need for getting our words in place before we work on our visual brand. So let's look at some brands that put all of this into practice.

In Part 2, we examined the success of Nike Air Jordans, Red Ants Pants, and Russell Brunson's Two Comma Club—three brands that have elevated the status of their product or offer and created a cult of personality associated with their brand.

Air Jordans have the benefit of being a tangible good. The intangible personality associated with the shoes—rebellious and elite—is nearly as strong of a presence as the physical shoes themselves. The greatness of Michael Jordan, his refusal to play by the rules, and his absolute dominance on the court elevated the shoes beyond a simple utilitarian purpose.

At Red Ants Pants, the product itself is a personification of the customer—built for hard work, strong, and adorable.

And then there's the Two Comma Club. The idea of two commas takes the concept of making $1,000,000 and makes it elite, aspirational, and totally tangible. The award plaques for this status are styled like platinum record awards, echoing the prestige of popular musicians who "go platinum." Every detail of the experience is designed to give it weight, honor, and allure.

In my business, my Rainmaker Residency programs are synonymous with a distinct red color, that's a little bit gritty and reminiscent of hard work and dirt. I've had strangers DM me that they saw a shirt that was "the Rainmaker color," so they bought it and sent it to me.

There are so many ways to personify your brand and give even an intangible service, product, or offer a weight, a personality, and a presence.

DRESSING YOUR IDENTITY

Let's elevate the identity you're going to market to make it irresistible, aspirational, and tangible.

How? You probably know by now that there's a process.

There are four areas you're going to turn to when dressing up and elevating your identity.

Identity Closet

Let's start with visualizing what your identity wears. This is where you want to think about what an item signifies. What are the associated status, vibes, and implications of different clothing and accessory options. You want to humanize this identity and think about it like a real, living person.

You also want to think about what elements elevate your identity. How does your identity stand apart from everyone else's? How is it aspirational and desirable? Status matters. When we look back to Part 2, we can bring this one back to Maslow's hierarchy of needs. Remember that once we've satisfied our customer's social needs—making them feel included in our group or community—we need to fulfill their self-esteem needs, which include respect, recognition, and status. It's not enough to just be part of the group, they need to be admired and respected.

When shopping your identity closet, what fits your identity?

Does your identity gravitate toward cozy sweaters, warm fuzzy socks, and Lululemon leggings?

Or is your identity busy selecting the perfect pair of tailored trousers to go with its crisp white button-down, blazer, and loafers?

> ### *Elevation Opportunity*
>
> Your identity may dress head-to-toe in luxury goods, presenting itself as a fully elevated, luxe option.
>
> Your identity may be more down to earth, in the perfect jeans with a gorgeous pair of classic Louboutin red-soled stilettos that act as a singularly elevated item.
>
> How you choose to elevate your identity depends on the overall tone you want to strike, and the desires of your audience. The elevated item may not be something expensive—bringing in an upgraded presence through a unique quality, like a one-of-a-kind pair of handcrafted earrings.

Identity Playlist

Identities have vibes and energy. What does your identity listen to? Does it jam out, relax, sing along, or mix it up?

Think about it this way: If your business had a theme song, what would it be?

Once you think of a theme song, choose a few other songs that complement and complete the vibe. If you really want to take this to the next level, create an identity playlist on Spotify and share the link with your identity community. (Fun side note—a designer on my team listens to music that reminds her of different clients when she's designing! Music has strong connections to our identities.)

> *Don't forget to download your Identity Marketing Playlist on page 36.*

> ## *Elevation Opportunity*
>
> Consider what the type of music your identity listens to says about their status.
>
> Do they want to be popular and well liked by the masses so they listen to Top 40 pop?
>
> Does your identity need to be seen as intellectual so they really dig experimental jazz or classical music?
>
> Or are they more into being seen as an individual so they listen to indie artists and lesser known, avant-garde bands?
>
> Each genre of music has its own brand of status and elevated meaning.

Identity Friend Group

Who does your identity hang out with? You are who you spend your time with, so your identity's friend group is crucial.

Your identity may hang out with new moms, online entrepreneurs, people from the local theater group, musicians, artists, travelers, or CEOs—it just depends on what crowd they are attracted to and where they fit in.

How does your identity carry themselves within their friend group? Are they the leader, the funny friend, the introspective one, the caretaker? Think about their dynamics within the group they hang with.

> ## *Elevation Opportunity*
>
> Which celebrities does your identity pal around with?
>
> Is your identity out and about with Taylor Swift and her girl squad, or enjoying Lake Como with George Clooney and Amal?
>
> Partying it up with Gigi and Bella Hadid or quietly enjoying the good life with Beyoncé?
>
> Elevate your identity's friend group by considering the celebrities they would be seen with and how they would look, feel, and act among those celebrities.
>
> This step will help you zero in on how status impacts the identity you've chosen to market.

Identity Space

Consider this an old-school MTV *Cribs* tour. Take us into your identity's home and show us around.

Where does your identity feel most at home and safe? Where is your identity comfortable?

Does your identity feel most at home in a showstopping, perfectly clean, professionally designed home, or are they more into a lived-in space filled with trinkets and treasures picked up from a lifetime of traveling?

Show us how your identity *lives*. This is one of the most humanizing aspects of dressing and personifying your identity.

> ### *Elevation Opportunity*
>
> Which rooms—outside of their own home—does your identity unlock? Is your identity comfortable navigating the inner circles of A-list celebrities' homes or is your identity most comfortable stepping into the living rooms of their family members?
>
> Consider both access and comfort at this point. Where does status take your identity?

Only once you have worked through finding, proving, naming, and dressing your identity are you ready to do identity-based branding and design.

Skipping over these four steps and jumping straight into designing your brand is just traditional brand design. We're doing something dramatically different. If you need a refresher on the difference in Identity Marketing and brand design, you can hop back to Part 1 and get clear on the nuanced (and crucial) difference.

Once you have worked through the Identity Code and successfully unlocked the proven identity you're ready to market, work through the end of this chapter with your designer or complete the visual identity steps yourself.

IDENTITY-BASED BRANDING AND DESIGN

- Logo
- Sublogo
- Color palette
- Fonts
- Mascot or character (optional)
- Patterns and textures
- Icons and badges
- Social media visuals
- Website design

Your visual brand—the images and elements that communicate your identity to your customers—includes things like:

Everything you create and share for your brand should reflect your new marketable identity.

Your visual brand is guided by specifics—what would your identity wear, how luxurious would it be, what colors define it—as well as a more general understanding of who your identity is and how they show up in the world.

Sharing your Identity Code discoveries with your designer can help them create an accurate mood board and a clear direction for your brand design.

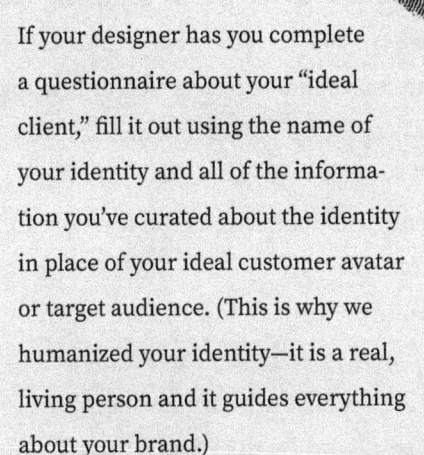

> *Pro Tip:*
>
> If your designer has you complete a questionnaire about your "ideal client," fill it out using the name of your identity and all of the information you've curated about the identity in place of your ideal customer avatar or target audience. (This is why we humanized your identity—it is a real, living person and it guides everything about your brand.)

You can incorporate your identity (by name and by design) into everything from your email signature to Instagram highlight covers, PowerPoint templates, your LinkedIn banner, and your marketing materials.

Once you've solidified your marketable identity, you will probably need to refresh or redesign your website to include your new identity-based branding. That's a perfect opportunity to work on a page for your identity hub as well as making sure every page on your website is written to and for your new identity.

Create a dedicated hub on your website that speaks directly to your customers about the identity and works as a community gathering spot. This is where you can post your identity's birth story and non-negotiables, as well as inviting your customers to participate in message boards, buy branded swag, access exclusive content only for your identity-adopters, and read features about members.

Anything short of a holistic brand, website design, and messaging overhaul will limit the efficacy and impact of your new identity.

You worked so hard to find it, prove it, name it, and dress it ... and now it's time to share it with the world!

WHAT'S NEXT?

This ends Part 3 and concludes the individual component of Identity Marketing. But we're not done yet! Part 4 is all about how to take your external marketable identity and apply it to your internal culture.

It's time to extend the concept of Identity beyond marketing and apply it to your leadership, your team, and your culture. Because your customers aren't the only ones suffering from an identity crisis ...

Identity Marketing Legends

We gathered some of our favorite Identity Marketing Legends and are sharing their stories and takeaways—from either the book, attending our Identity Marketing Intensive, or intuitively following Identity Marketing principles on their own—with you here. Read through their experiences, breakthroughs, and lessons learned to get inspired and see what Identity Marketing is doing for real brands and businesses ... no matter what you sell or the size of your budget!

LAURA BELGRAY
FOUNDER OF TALKING SHRIMP

Laura Belgray is a copywriting expert who helps entrepreneurs and personal brands find the perfect words to express and sell what they do. She also writes the best emails. So why did Laura name her copywriting business Talking Shrimp, of all things? There's no meaningful story behind the name itself: she chose it when her CPA told her she and her husband needed an S-Corp to save on taxes. Her husband works in the restaurant world, hence the shrimp, and her work is all about words, so in came the talking.

But Laura Belgray is an Identity Marketing Legend because of the story and context she built *after* Talking Shrimp was born. She took a random name and gave it context and meaning, creating a legion of loyal fans who happily call themselves "Shrimpers."

She started referring to her email audience as "Shrimpers," and it caught on. People loved feeling like they were part of her community, along with her direct, hilarious, sarcastic emails. Anyone joining her email list can be a Shrimper – tens of thousands of people are. But the next level involves joining her intimate mastermind Shrimp Club. These Shrimpers are in the inner circle, and there's an understanding that they are the *real* Shrimpers.

Laura turned a name without meaning into one of the most desirable identities on the internet by creating a community that felt personally connected to her, initially through her raw, honest storytelling in emails and eventually through personal connections and 1:1 time with her in Shrimp Club.

The best thing Identity Marketing did for Laura Belgray: Identity marketing gave Laura the ability to create an aspirational community by offering an invitation to become something unexpected—a Shrimper. She was able to retrofit her invitation to an off-the-wall name, intentionally build out the context and meaning of the name after the fact, and establish a committed community.

ADELAIDE OLGUIN
FOUNDER OF TALKBOX.MOM

Adelaide Olguin and her team at TalkBox.Mom had to find a way to disrupt a crowded market of language learning programs, and they did. By focusing on families learning together, starting out on a path of fluency instead of focusing on grammar rules and vocab memorization, TalkBox.Mom was able to build a thriving business.

When she stepped into the Identity Marketing Intensive, Adelaide had been thinking about the identity of her ideal customers for a while. She knew there was more she wanted to invite them to be a part of, but she didn't have the words for it ... yet.

Adelaide's breakthrough came when she and her team started combing through her customer testimonials during Day 1 of the Identity Marketing Intensive. One thing that stood out was the thing families were excited about and, ultimately, why they loved TalkBox.Mom: FLUENCY. They loved being able to speak and feeling like they had an accurate command of the language.

Despite "mom" being in the company name, it really was and always had been the family identity above all others that permitted her buyers to invest. – The identity of "Fluency Families" was born! It's both an invitation to *learn* in a different way than any other program (fluency vs. memorization or grammar) and to become something aspirational ... a family of fluent foreign language speakers!

The best thing Identity Marketing did for Adelaide Olguin: Identity Marketing gave Adelaide and her team at TalkBox.Mom a clear way to disrupt a super saturated market and generate serious revenue. Inviting language learners to become a Fluency Family is such a different invitation than anything Duolingo or Rosetta Stone can offer – and families are responding to the call!

MO FAUL

SOUL-POWERED EXECUTIVE AND CAREER COACH

Coach Mo has been a successful career coach for over a decade, helping women in the corporate space where there's a common, shared belief that in order to get ahead, you have to sell out. But Coach Mo's *whole approach* is the opposite. She helps women find their dream jobs and land serious promotions by tapping into the power of their souls instead of selling them.

Identity Marketing helped Coach Mo sharpen her message and lean more heavily into the concept of what it means to be a "soul-powered woman". She turned up the volume on inviting women to participate in Soul-Powered Career Coaching and developed a strong presence in the space through her podcast *Soul-Powered Revolution*.

As she worked through the Identity Code, she kept coming back to the concept of non-negotiables and how crucial these are to the identity of her soul-powered ideal client. She was able to clearly define that a soul-powered career woman unsubscribes from the inequalities—pay inequality, gender inequality, power inequality—that make her feel like she has to sell her soul in order to get ahead.

The best thing Identity Marketing did for Coach Mo: It gave her a path to the innermost *truth* in her messaging so she could unapologetically show up for the soul-powered women she coaches and better help her clients get to the full truth of who *they* are.

DR. JORDIN WIGGINS
NATUROPATHIC DOCTOR AND PLEASURE + INTIMACY COACH AT THE PLEASURE COLLECTIVE

Dr. Jordin helps high-achieving, alpha women learn how to be as much of a badass in the bedroom and relationships as they are in business. Before she came to the Identity Marketing Intensive, she struggled with her marketing, even though she had invested multiple-six figures in marketing coaches and strategies they never felt aligned.

Getting serious about her clients' identity helped her reconnect with why she wrote her book *The Pink Canary* and started her business in the first place. Identity Marketing led her back to the woman she was supposed to be talking to—someone who was at the beginning of her Pleasure Path—instead of the woman much further down the path that she had been trying to market to.

Recognizing that the women she wanted to work with hold tightly to their identity as High Achievers and don't want to give up that identity, she had to create an even more compelling identity for her clients to aspire to. The idea of inviting her high achiever clients to become empowered Receivers made perfect sense. Her marketing strategy was clear: invite High Achievers to work through the pleasure path to become Receivers. This made marketing not only feel aligned, but *fun* again!

The best thing Identity Marketing did for Dr. Jordin Wiggins: Identity marketing clearly outlined the phases of identity her clients go through so she could speak clearly and authentically to them. It made marketing feel fun again and gave her team exactly what they needed to speak directly to their ideal clients.

SARA WALKA
CEO OF THE SISTERS ENCHANTED

Sara started The Sisters Enchanted with her actual sister, Anna. They teach women how to journal and manifest all sorts of things so they can transform midlife women who are at a crossroads into confident women whose lives feel like magic.

In the beginning, Sara was set on being clever and inviting her customers to be Magic Maker. She put it in emails, used it on social, and essentially tried to force Magic Maker to happen. But it never caught on! Later, when Sara came to the Identity Marketing Intensive, she took "Enchanted Sister" to her community in the "Prove It" step and discovered that was *exactly* what her people wanted to be called!

They wanted to be an Enchanted Sister. The call to join the sisterhood was what they were responding to after all this time. There was no need to be overly clever—Sara and Anna had done a better job with identity marketing from the beginning than they even realized.

The best thing Identity Marketing did for Sara Walka: Identity Marketing gave Sara *proof* that she had already tapped into the identity her audience wanted to be called to join. It helped her accept the obvious instead of trying to complicate things and create something totally new when Enchanted Sisters was *already* a compelling identity for her customers!

TAMSEN WEBSTER
PART KEYNOTE SPEAKER, PART MESSAGE STRATEGIST

Tamsen Webster helps people change how they see and what they do. Identity is at the very core of her transformational work – she's been an Identity Marketing Legend long before there was even a term for it.

One of the coolest things Tamsen teaches and uses in her work with massive organizations is that the only way humans operate over the long term is to act in line with our internal logic. And our identity—the way we see ourselves and the way we want to be seen—is a core part of that internal logic.

She teaches and reinforces one of the main drivers of identity marketing: If you're not connecting your services and offers to your clients' internal logic, you're missing out on the very reasons they would stay with you for the long run. (Remember the loyal fans and legendary brand I promised you? This is the psychology behind why it works!)

The best thing Identity Marketing did for Tamsen Webster: Identity Marketing and the psychological theories behind it perfectly align with her work, her keynotes, and her newest book, *Say What They Can't Unhear.*

DANIELLE CONNOR
BRAND + WEBSITE DESIGNER

Danielle Connor designs Million-Dollar Websites™ for high-achieving, successful female-founded businesses. Her entire job is creating a true, authentic representation of her clients: she literally helps people create their own brand identity. So when she stepped into an Identity Marketing Intensive and heard me telling her that Identity

Marketing isn't about the owner, it's about the client ... and that it comes *before* brand identity ... she felt some understandable pushback.

She's an incredible high achiever, so she worked through her questions and showed up to fully participate in the two-day experience. Everything about her personal experience and the ethos of her business led her to wanting to invite her customers to join her "squad." It tracked with her past experience as a cheerleader and had a strong correlation to how she shows up as her clients' biggest cheerleader in their business.

But she was committed to the process, and in Part 2 of the Identity Code when she polled her audience about the identity (validation, baby!), there were two different identities resonating with her people. Danielle sat down with the super insightful data she could gather in just a few hours (we're really into working smarter, not harder) and saw there were two identities her community was into: being a squad and being a sorority.

Danielle is still in the process of working through the "Name It" step as she works through the data she was able to mine from her community and testing out what her overall audience will resonate with most. But regardless of the name she lands on, she's working with a better depth of understanding and has more context for building out a community her audience is obsessed with being part of.

The best thing Identity Marketing did for Danielle Connor: It gave her a tool and framework for stepping into her own power and being able to play BIG. She found it so validating to realize "it's not just a website." She's creating a community that has the power to lift people up and change the world ... all thanks to Identity Marketing.

VITTORIA DAELLI
LAUNCH MARKETER + FUNNEL DESIGNER

Vittoria is incredibly talented at helping others see what they can't see themselves. But when it came to her own work? That task felt a bit more challenging.

After attending the Identity Marketing Intensive, she felt herself experiencing a full-on identity crisis. Instead of giving in or giving up, she kept circling on the mantra that summed up who she is and what she does: "Stop being afraid of your own brilliance."

Turns out, instead of seeing her brilliance as a problem to be solved, she just needed to look at it with a new perspective and treat her brilliance as the solution. This shift—brought on by her work during the Identity Marketing Intensive—led to Vittoria opening up her coffee chat calendar to her email list instead of pitching a new Black Friday offer. The result? A full calendar of conversations that reminded her why she does the work she does in the first place and a strong, permanent shift in perspective.

The best thing Identity Marketing did for Vittoria Daelli: It gave her permission and space to lean into who she *really* is, which in turn led to her creating a safe, inspiring space for others to process and acknowledge their own authentic, brilliant selves.

CASEY LIGHTBODY
FOUNDER + CEO OF THE QUIET COLLECTIVE

Casey Lightbody started with a mission to help introverts succeed in business, but she quickly noticed a concerning pattern—her message was attracting people who were using the "introvert" label as an excuse to stay stuck rather than as a strength to embrace. She knew something needed to change.

Her first breakthrough came when she discovered the profound dual meaning of "quiet." There was the quiet personalities of introverts, sensitives, and empaths, but there was also something deeper: the transformative power of quietening the inner noise to hear the whispers of intuition. This understanding revealed that true quiet was about a deep connection to self through listening to those intuitive whispers, connecting to others through meaningful relationships, and connecting to the world through purposeful impact.

It was this foundation that Casey brought into her Identity Marketing journey. As she dove deep into hours of sales call transcripts and conducted extensive polls with her ideal clients, she was specifically looking to understand how this connection-driven approach to quiet resonated with her audience. The research revealed something surprising and powerful: The people who most embodied this dual meaning of quiet weren't just *any* introverts or sensitive souls. They were high-achieving leaders who had already discovered what Casey had been uncovering—that their quiet nature was actually their leadership superpower. This led to the powerful identity of "Quiet Leaders," women who lead with intention, thoughtfulness, and deep impact rather than noise.

The best thing Identity Marketing did for Casey: It helped her discover and define the "Quiet Leader" identity through systematic research and validation, transforming The Quiet Collective into a powerful movement that mobilizes women to do business, life, and leadership differently. The process helped her attract and empower the *right* people.

MARY CZARNECKI
SPEAKER, CONSULTANT, ANA FACULTY MEMBER, AND FOUNDER OF MARYCZARNECKISPEAKS.COM AND STICKY NOTE MARKETING

Mary Czarnecki helps marketers, creatives, and business leaders communicate their ideas in a way that actually gets people to listen and act. Through her speaking, workshops, and consulting, she equips professionals with tools grounded in storytelling, neuroscience, and real-world strategy to simplify the process of communicating in a way that connects and delivers real impact.

Before attending the Identity Marketing

Intensive, Mary knew her audience wanted to stand out and lead with confidence, but she hadn't yet connected their shared aspirations to a deeper identity. Her breakthrough came during the Intensive when she realized the power of inviting her audience into a shared mission: To become Sticky Notables (or "Notables"), professionals who communicate in a way that captivates stakeholders and inspires action ... marketers who stand out in a noisy world and confidently lead their teams with clarity and creativity.

The Identity Marketing framework didn't just help Mary craft a name; it gave her the clarity and confidence to build a community where marketers see themselves as bold, unforgettable communicators. This identity has become a rallying cry for professionals who are ready to lead with clarity, purpose, and impact. Now she's not just teaching marketers how to write creative briefs or build campaigns. She's helping them step into a new identity as bold, unforgettable communicators.

The best thing Identity Marketing did for Mary Czarnecki: It helped her transform her audience into a community of action-takers who proudly wear the identity of Sticky Notables—professionals who stand out, inspire action, and make ideas stick even in a noisy, distracted world.

MANJA HORNER
LEARNING CONSULTANCY CEO

Manja supports business managers of trades unions, so she targets a very specific person. Before coming to the Identity Marketing Intensive, she didn't see her target buyer clearly.

During the workshop, she realized that so many of the new managers she was working with were really overwhelmed. They came to their work as tradespeople without specific leadership or management skills, but they wanted to do their best and prove themselves as a leaders.

The Identity Marketing Intensive helped Manja come up with the idea to create a union leaders' club or network where she could help the newly appointed managers embrace their role while learning leadership skills and networking with their colleagues. The market research she conducted allowed her to better conceptualize how they spend their free time and what feels like a reward, so she was able to construct a safe, appealing space for union leaders.

The best thing Identity Marketing did for Manja Horner: It crystalized exactly who her decision maker and buyer is, turning them from an idea into something that felt distinctly human. She was able to clearly see what her target buyer needed and wanted, giving her a clear path to developing a safe space for them.

BECOME AN IDENTITY MARKETING LEGEND IN TWO DAYS!

*Learn how you can uncover your brand's marketable identity and bring it to life by visiting: **youridentitymarketing.com**.*

This is your chance to master the 4-step Identity Code™ framework and forever shift your marketing from "buy this" to "be this"!

PART FOUR:

Leveraging Identity Beyond Marketing and Sales

CHAPTER FIFTEEN

The Cure *for* the Labor Force Crisis

How to raise the stakes for those inside your business without expensive benefits or massive signing bonuses

Your consumers aren't the only ones having a crisis.

The labor force serving those consumers is suffering from the same overwhelming confusion: "Who the heck am I?" "What am I doing here?"

The post-COVID labor force landscape has been bleak.

We're facing labor shortages and worker displacement, with many industries—like hospitality, retail, and healthcare—going through severe labor shortages. Remote work has allowed many employees to leave cities, leaving critical labor gaps in fields where in-person work is required.

The post-COVID employee demands flexibility and expects the option to work remotely at least part of the time. When tech giant Dell told their employees they had to return to office if they wanted to be eligible for any future promotions, nearly 50 percent chose to stay remote and give up their eligibility.[43] People are more interested in remote work options than increased pay.

The so-called Great Resignation following COVID-19 saw employees resign en masse after re-evaluating their priorities during the pandemic. Many decided that low-paying or high-stress jobs simply weren't worth it.[44]

And then there's the "quiet quitting" phenomenon, where employees don't actually resign, but intentionally do as little as possible to remain employed. They never exceed expectations or put in more than the bare minimum of effort.

As Gen Z enters the workforce, leaders must adjust to a whole new perspective on work. Gen Z has expectations of increased social responsibility, diversity, equity, and inclusion, and a strong desire for work that serves a bigger purpose.

Feeling defeated yet?

The post-COVID workforce looks like:
- Talented team members leaving in droves
- Remaining workers not producing like they used to
- Company leaders struggling to reignite passion and productivity
- Everyone—from the CEO to the interns—feeling completely burned out

This is bad enough for leaders in traditional spaces, and *doubly* as hard for anyone who is in the position of rainmaker—sales people, marketers, and business owners—who are responsible for generating direct revenue.

The numbers don't lie.

83 percent of marketing professionals report that they are burned out.[45]

Chief Marketing Officers (CMOs) have the shortest tenure level in the C-suite.[46]

Companies are losing $210,000+ every three years thanks to CMO turnover.

Experienced marketing professionals are overloaded and under-supported, leading to high levels of burnout and increased turnover. This impacts marketers at all levels, but especially at the top. CMOs are quickly becoming an endangered species.

This doesn't just affect people at the top. All team members from marketing, sales, fulfillment and customer service, cross-functional partners, agencies, and yes, the customer too, are negatively impacted by marketing burnout and turnover.

In a previous role, I stepped in to lead a marketing team that had been through *four leaders in less than two years*. Imagine the dynamics at play, and the loss of productivity caused by such disruptive leadership changes. And this is happening in teams and departments that are directly responsible for generating revenue.

SO WHAT'S THE ANSWER?

It's not investing more resources in more expensive benefits or luring the best people with a lucrative signing bonus. Spending more money isn't going to get you the passionate, committed workforce you need. Top performers don't really care if you have a Ping-Pong table or if you give them free snacks, if they can't align who they are within the company's identity.
In the first three parts of this book, we focused on replacing the invitation to your customers of "buy this" with the more powerful and effective "be this."

In Part 4, we explore how to invite your employees not just to work for you, but to *be* the company, aligning their own identities with your company's identity.

We unlock the key to creating an identity-based culture that empowers top talent to perform at the highest level and never want to leave.

All of our identity work up to this point has been external, focused on our customers. Now, we turn the lens inward and take up an internal examination of identity as it applies to your workforce in your company, team, and culture.

When you leverage the power of internal identity, organizations—from the smallest to the largest—can build teams who are so passionate and committed that they will want to:

- Celebrate their employment like a personal achievement.
- Carry out the company vision as if it were their own.
- Tattoo the company logo on their skin.

I've been a Marketer for over seventeen years, and I've seen it all—the brilliant, the dismal, the effective, the utter failures, and everything in between. At the end of the day, I believe:

> The true magic of marketing lies in the hands of visionary leaders, not just in the strategies and tactics they employ.

That belief is the reason I could not, in good conscience, deliver the first three parts of this book without also addressing the leaders who are implementing the power of Identity Marketing across their organizations.

LEADERSHIP, TEAMS, AND COMPANY CULTURE

In these final three chapters, I'm going to walk you through how to use Identity Marketing to improve your leadership, your team, and your culture. We'll start with how Identity Marketing applies to each level of an organization.

Individual Identity

Individual identity, your identity as a leader, is how you perceive yourself within your organization. Individual leaders look to their role, values, career goals, and personal branding to see how they align with the company's mission and culture.

When we talk about leadership, we're talking specifically about how you as a leader use Identity Marketing to enhance your individual identity. Your identity impacts your personal job satisfaction, your career development, and how your employees perform.

Team Identity

Team identity, or the identity of a specific team within an organization, is the collective sense of belonging and shared purpose among members of a team or department. This is a group identity, driven by how team members perceive themselves as part of a cohesive unit working together to reach shared goals.

This shared identity affects the team's cohesion, productivity, and ability to achieve its common objectives. The team's identity isn't necessarily the same as the broader company culture, which is one reason some teams are more successful than others within the same organization.

Company Culture

Company culture, unlike the individual or team identities, applies to the entire organization. Culture is made up of shared values, beliefs, behaviors, and practices that are more or less consistent across the company. This identity is focused on how employees perceive the company, how the company operates as a whole, and how it is viewed by external stakeholders.

Organizational identity (a.k.a. company culture) includes the internal and external brand. When there's a significant disconnect between the company's external brand and its internal brand, things can get dicey. (I share a story about how disastrous this can be in Chapter 19.)

The workforce (just like your customer) has been facing a serious identity crisis. The next three chapters explain how leaders can address this crisis and put the power of Identity Marketing to work across different levels of an organization.

CHAPTER SIXTEEN

Identity-Based Leadership

How to improve your leadership without investing another dollar in professional development

You can't be a good leader unless you first identify as a good leader.

Let's unpack that because it's not as simple as it seems.

From the time you are born, you learn how to show up, as an individual contributor. You develop skills at being responsible for your own choices, behaviors, and results, and you become comfortable in your role.

But when you step into leadership, suddenly, the identity you've always possessed is thrown out.

You must assume a new identity as a leader. Now your success is based on how well you help other individual contributors achieve their greatest potential and generate the greatest results. You're not in direct control of your outcomes anymore.

You can't force your team members to perform the way you need them to. It can be a terrifying realization, especially for high achievers who are used to doing whatever it takes to win.

As a leader, your responsibility increases, while your direct focus of control decreases, requiring you to fully embrace your new identity. If you want to be a leader who lasts.

FROM CEO TO VISIONARY

Let me tell you a little story about the importance of understanding and accepting your identity as a leader.

It all started with me wanting to help CEOs and marketers work better together. So many CEOs I consulted with tended to limit, restrict, and even resent their marketing leaders (or marketing team). The CEO conflated the marketers role with their own, so when the marketer was successful it felt like they were directly competing with the

CEO. I decided to use my dual identity—as a CEO *and* a Marketer—to create a program that would bridge this huge gap I saw in otherwise thriving organizations.

In my own Rainmaker Residency Plus program, I invited CEOs to transition from full-time *marketer* to full-time *visionary* of their business. This transformation meant handing over the launches, funnels, ads, and team, to a marketing leader. This letting go would free the CEO (a.k.a. the visionary) to finally lead from out front, while the marketer (a.k.a. the Rainmaker) made it rain behind the scenes.

There are not one but two identity upgrades involved in this process.

Let's start with the CEOs.

Their perception of being *the CEO* was already subsumed in their tendency to be "chief *everything* officers." There was no way to powerfully rebrand the title of CEO because the title itself defined the exact problem we were trying to solve. CEOs needed to stop being the chief everything officer and become something more—focused on owning and executing their vision—instead of doing the daily tasks and responsibilities involved with running a business.

So the CEOs got a huge identity upgrade to Visionary.

The title encompassed everything they were supposed to be focusing on, but without leaving room for all the marketing responsibilities and metrics. Stepping into a new role as the visionary gave overworked, stuck-in-marketing CEOs permission (and the responsibility) to be the keeper and messenger of their corporate vision as their core responsibility and corresponding KPI (key performance indicator).

Here's where the psychology of loss aversion comes into play. This principle states that humans are more sensitive to the idea of losing something than the prospect of gaining something. I couldn't just yank away their beloved Marketer-CEO identity and tell them to do better. I had to create a new, more desirable, *bigger* identity—the visionary—for them to step into.

When applying this concept to your own identity as a leader, you must find something to aspire to that's better than the current identity you embody. If "visionary" resonates with you and aligns to your responsibilities, feel free to take it and use it! If it's not the right fit, dig in and find a title that encompasses your identity as a leader. Don't just think about the name. Make sure to consider the meaning behind the title, just like we did when working through the Identity Code.

Another key element of helping CEOs transition to and become visionaries was their new key performance indicators. How can you gauge your success if you don't have data to track? This is where I introduced the visionary KPI: the number of times you, the visionary, share the company's mission and vision as the public spokesperson of your organization.

The truth about most CEOs I've worked with is that they were resentful of marketers who came in and excelled, because it felt like the new marketer was doing the CEO's job, better than they could do it themselves. I've personally witnessed talented marketers get blamed, yelled at, and ultimately fired because they did too good of a job and offended the CEO, who had not relinquished their identity as the original revenue-generator of the company.

A huge part of the new identity involved giving up their chokehold on the marketing strategies and KPIs, not because they weren't brilliant marketers, but because they were past that stage in their business. Their identity had outgrown marketing and was bigger than championing revenue-generating tasks. This was done strategically and intentionally, so the marketers could step in and do *their* jobs.

In order to promote the marketers to their rightful place, I had to invite the CEOs to step out of the way and completely change the way they saw themselves, measured their success, and identified themselves as a leader.

Once that was done, I needed a new identity for the marketers to assume so they would feel the weight and responsibility of their new role, without the presence of the CEO hanging around and taking care of things like before.

Why didn't I choose "head of marketing," "VP of marketing," or "marketing director"? Because title inflation is very real and those titles are virtually meaningless in small, privately owned companies. We care about the context and story behind the title. The commonly used marketing titles were overused, overinflated, and had become completely devoid of purpose or meaning.

I didn't want to call them chief marketing officers, because they were already replacing the CEO. Throwing in a new C-suite title felt like setting them up for failure with their newly promoted visionaries. So I called them Rainmakers.

Rainmakers get things done. They have serious charisma, a decent dose of swagger, and they've earned it all because they make it rain.

Individual leader identity was the cornerstone of the successful Rainmaker Residency Plus program. Giving CEOs a new identity and promoting them out of their "chief everything officer" capacity gave them a new way to understand their role and track their success, while simultaneously giving marketers the ability to step into their Rainmaker identities and generate revenue without internal (and often subconscious) sabotage.

WHAT'S IN A NAME?

Back in the early 2000s, renowned marketing legend Ann Handley gave herself the title of "chief content officer."[47]

In a world of inflated titles and worn out "chiefs," this was a novelty. It had never been used before, and Handley took charge of her career and gave it to herself. She didn't initially see the self-assumed title as a way to elevate her career. Instead, it was her attempt to elevate what she did—content.

Back in 1997, she founded a company called ClickZ.com. Its purpose was to help businesses figure out how to use a nascent thing called the internet to help with their marketing. It was one of the first sources of digital marketing information.

While it seems commonplace and unthinkable to *not* use the internet for marketing now, "Like *Friends*, in 1997 it was a very revolutionary idea! People barely knew what an email address was," Handley told me in a podcast interview.

Although Handley was the founder of the company, she wasn't clear on what her day-to-day *job* was going to be. She focused on content, but titles like "executive editor" didn't feel like they gave content the modern, groundbreaking status it deserved. She headed up all the content that was teaching businesses how to market online, so she dubbed herself the chief content officer as a signal that content was important enough to demand a chief—like finance or operations.

Ann Handley eventually sold ClickZ, but brought the title of chief content officer with her when she joined a new venture a few years later:

> *"As far as I know, I am the world's first chief content officer. I made up that title. It goes back to 1997, and I don't know anybody who had the title before I did."*

Even into the early 2000s, Handley said she would hand out her business card that people would misread her title, thinking she was in charge of happiness instead of content—what's driving the web and becoming the way we communicate online.

She intended to elevate the art and craft of what she worked in—content—and she did. But she also gave herself a new identity to live up to. Without even knowing it, Handley was following through with Step 3 of the Identity Code: dressing up her title with meaning, context, and a powerful backstory that gave it weight.

Her style and work gave this title meaning and context. By becoming a Chief Content Officer, she elevated the art of content and herself by extension. The concept that content was "chief" was obvious to Handley, but the concept that she was the chief took longer to take root.

When describing how it took her much longer to feel like the chief herself compared to feeling confident in the content as something that deserved a chief, Handley said:

> "I had to get there myself. It [chief of content role] was more than what I was publishing and producing—it was who I was."

Handley, through giving herself a new, aspirational identity, found that the title elevated content's importance *and* elevated the role of the leader in charge of it.

THE ROI (RETURN ON INVESTMENT) OF IDENTITY-BASED LEADERSHIP

Believing you are a leader and giving yourself a title that's imbued with meaning, context, and power isn't just about feeling up to the task, or giving you the confidence to stand out and shine.

Identity-based leadership changes everything about how you operate, how you see yourself, and what you achieve.

Business coach Heather Chauvin came into the Rainmaker Residency thinking she needed someone to join her team to solve her marketing problem. She anticipated that hiring a full-time Rainmaker would solve all of her problems.

Through some trial and error, Chauvin realized she couldn't rely on someone else to solve her problems. She had to become the type of leader who didn't just execute her visions, but intentionally led and developed team members who were brought in and aligned with her vision as well.

She thought she was showing up as a leader by taking risks and making hiring decisions, but that only put her cash flow at risk and endangered her organization's success. It wasn't until she accepted and embodied her identity as a *people leader* that things started to fall into place.

After walking through this experience and figuring out her true identity, Heather shared this reflection with me in a private Voxer (voice messaging app) message:

> *"Today I was reflecting on the ROI of being in your world. And the inner leadership stuff has really been the game changer. Who I've become just because I had to ... I'm a product of just being in your energy and listening to you."*

You may never see the fullest return on your investment in professional development, team hires, or other leadership strategies until you embrace identity-based leadership.

HOW TO IMPROVE YOUR IDENTITY AS A LEADER

If you're ready to step up your identity-based leadership game, there are a few actions and resources that will help you on your way.

Titles matter, but they are not limited to what's given to you. What really matters is the title you give yourself.

Whether you're in a position to literally change your title or not, it's time to find a title with meaning and context that inspires you to become the leader you want to be. And remember, you don't have to be in a defined leadership role to start becoming the leader you want to be.

Upgrade your job description. No matter what role you fill, you should have a written out, concrete job description that reflects the deeper meaning of your leadership identity.

CHAPTER SEVENTEEN

The Identity-Based Team

How to give your team a competitive edge, without coercion, fear, or monetary rewards

The team leader's identity and sense of self directly impacts the individual contributors on the team, creating a unique identity for different teams within the same department or organization.

In teams with multiple levels of leadership, the identity of the team can shift and change at each level of management, depending on the immediate manager and the leaders above them. Changing a team's identity can be incredibly difficult for a few reasons.

1. The team is made up of many individuals with different experiences, perspectives, and values.

2. Levels of leadership above the immediate leader can directly or indirectly influence the team's identity and self-perception.

3. Buy-in can be hard to get, especially when team members are suspicious of intent and resistant to change.

When you can find an identity that is collectively aspirational for each member of the team, you can unlock unprecedented results and lock-in your best talent for years to come. Pitch it in an engaging, enticing manner, and get team members excited about embracing it.

REBUILDING CRUMBLING TEAMS

I took a job as chief of staff at a company I was thrilled to work for. On the outside, it was a women's empowerment organization that was bold, successful, and unapologetic. They were known and mentioned by A-list celebrities and had millions of followers on Instagram.

I thought these were my people. This was my kind of business. And then I stepped behind the scenes.

As I got the lay of the land, I realized that this organization might outwardly champion women and their success, but internally it was an empowerment contradiction run by two owners managing two distinct sides of the business. As a result, the smaller teams were completely out of sync. Half the company felt like one business while the other half felt like a completely different business.

The first time I met the owners in person was when they flew me out to LA to collaborate with them as they worked through their brand identity with a consultant. One of the first things I heard as we sat down at the table to begin the process was that one of the owners hated a specific word.

The word she hated? It was the name of her own company.

It was then that I realized the owner was experiencing a personal identity crisis of her own. If I had any hope of improving the overall company culture, I would need to shield the team from what was happening at the top and focus on improving company culture at the team level.

The problem? Identity work only *really* sticks

if it starts from the top and is adopted down the ranks.

The leader was not willing or in a position to do the identity work that needed to be done for a complete company culture overhaul, so all I could do was lead from my position and focus on changing the identity of each team, one at a time.

I started with the operations team and quickly landed on calling us the "mamacitas." This name struck a chord for several reasons. We had the most mothers in our team of the whole company, and as a whole, we saw ourselves as the mothers of our paying customers.

It was our job to nurture them, make them feel seen. We would soothe their tears, calm their complaints, and assure them of their investments. As soon as our disheveled ops team became the mamacitas, we started working together more cohesively. The existing team members took a new pride in their role.

The name had some spicy Latina-infused flair and elevated the group from "operations" to caregivers of the customers, solvers of the problems, and mothers of the organization.

Once I had re-identified the ops team and watched the mamacitas step into their new, unified purpose, I moved on to the marketing team.

This was the most mismanaged, dysfunctional team in the organization. They had gone through four heads of marketing in less than a year, and I stepped on board as the fifth.

The entire team was struggling, so I knew we needed something to pick us up quickly. Here was the issue: I needed a name that would both resuscitate deflated marketers on the team while also being attractive and aspirational to the incredible new talent the team desperately needed.

We couldn't have a name that screamed "We need help!" without scaring off the new people, but I didn't want to create a new identity for incoming members that would alienate the existing team.

I quickly decided to rename our team, and our Slack channel, as "rainmakers" (you may remember that from my signature program in the previous chapter) and it worked. Part of the magic of the rainmakers title was that I excluded anyone outside of our team from the Slack channel. Rainmakers only.

It stuck.

ASSERTING YOUR IMPORTANCE

If you lead a team that is looked down upon or undervalued within the organization, giving your team a new identity is one of the best ways to stake your claim and let others know your team matters.

Years ago, I led the SEO + PPC (search engine optimization and pay-per-click) team at a property management software company. We rendered services to clients while everyone else at the company was software based. It was obvious that our team was the exception, and it felt like we were seriously undervalued by leadership.

As the only service offering in the entire company, led by a CEO who was very vocal about his distaste and disinterest in anything service based, we were kind of out there on our own.

I knew we needed to embrace our unique identity within the company if we were ever going to make serious progress. So we adopted "Started from the Bottom," by Drake—a song about rising from the bottom to the top of the game—as our theme song.

We continued to "dress" our identity by creating huge visual representations of our revenue and campaign goals, that we aggressively tracked in our shared office space. And somehow along the way, we started wearing wilderness shirts featuring wolves and other wild animals on Wednesdays because we were wild.

Our underdog team banded together in our pursuit of becoming champions. We wore our howling wolf shirts with pride. And we reached our massive goals, with our success displayed for everyone in the office to see.

Sometimes leaning into the stereotypes or judgments about your team can be the best way to motivate your team members and create an aspirational identity out of the undesirable.

SOMETIMES YOUR TEAM NAMES THEMSELVES

As a team leader, it may be up to you to create a new identity, source a name that embodies that identity, and get your team to buy in and adopt it. This is typically the case.

But sometimes, your team channels your energy and names themselves. A team-assigned identity is the strongest, because it came from within: an organic expression of the internal identity.

This is what happened with my current team.

One of my clients started referring to me as "Veyoncé" (a play on Beyoncé) when I would speak my mind and get fired up about different topics. One of my team members latched onto the concept of Veyoncé and dubbed our team the "V-hive." (Beyoncé's fans call themselves the Beyhive.)

My team members look up to me as a mentor and powerful supporter of their businesses, dreams, and goals. To them, being part of the "V-hive" feels like an embodiment of the compassion, respect, and status they enjoy from working with me.

Whether you name your team, or your team names themselves, or you arrive at an identity by some happy convergence of the two, an aspirational, aligned identity will make the team more productive, more satisfied, and more fulfilled.

IMPROVE YOUR TEAM'S IDENTITY

Giving your team an identity is one of the best ways to pull everyone together and channel their energy and efforts in specific, productive ways.

It may feel like all you need to do is pick a catchy name and that will do the trick, but it's really the context behind the name that holds the power.

We went over the process in Part 3, so make sure you follow the Identity Code process if you want your team's identity to be meaningful and motivating.

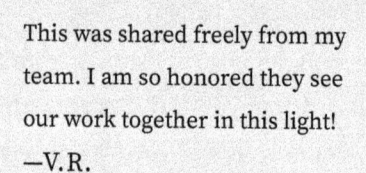

> *Author Note:*
>
> This was shared freely from my team. I am so honored they see our work together in this light!
> —V.R.

CHAPTER EIGHTEEN

The Identity-Based Organization

How to build a strong, passionate culture without being cheesy or lame

Most people would argue that organizational culture comes first and trickles down to impact teams and individuals. But that's not how I see it actually working in the hundreds of organizations I have supported, or the dream teams I've architected.

Organizational culture is built from the ground up, starting with people who know themselves and expanding to teams who have a cohesive, collective identity that is aligned with who they are and what they want to be.

Culture is the result of strong individuals who know themselves, and teams that are unified in their identity.

There are many misconceptions about culture in the workplace these days. We see organizations that think they can slap a slogan on a letterhead and call it culture or that believe benefits like unlimited PTO (paid time off) or mental health support count.

Identity-based culture is a real commitment. It gets infused into every aspect of the organization, from the individual contributor roles to teams, management, and the C-suite. It's a natural result of hiring people who align with the greater mission and vision of the company. They buy into the importance of their contribution, and are committed to shared goals and purpose.

WHY DOES CULTURE MATTER?

Culture isn't an add-on benefit or an afterthought. Or at least it shouldn't be.

A strong, identity-based culture improves employee engagement and retention, helping your team members feel satisfied, motivated, and committed. This has the dual benefit of keeping top performers on your team and reducing turnover costs.

If you want to attract the best talent, having an attractive, real culture is one of the best recruitment tools.

Positive culture also improves your reputation and brand image. Gen Z employees entering the workforce have a focus on purpose-driven work. Millennials prioritize diversity and inclusion. Having a company culture that's built on integrity, equity, and respect, you're more likely to be perceived as a positive force in the community by potential employees.

If you're not motivated by the internal benefits of a positive, identity-based culture, you may be more interested in the external effects. Organizations with a positive culture tend to have better customer service and more sustainable, long-term success.

JUST DO IT

We've already looked at how Nike excels at external, customer Identity Marketing. They are truly a double threat, because they knock it out of the park with their internal identity, too.

Nike spelled backward is "Ekin," and this is what Nike superfans call themselves. This tradition apparently started in the 1990s when Ekins would tattoo the well known "swoosh" on their calves.[48] The practice continues to this day, with employees who feel closely connected to the company choosing to have the company's logo or an iteration of their legendary sneakers permanently inked on their bodies.

This commitment is a clear sign that Nike's external identity aligns so directly with their employees' identities that they want to show it to the world.

What would it take to build a culture at your organization that not only attracted top talent and kept workers performing their best, but made employees want to get a tattoo of your logo?

THE HUNK PHILOSOPHY

One of the most successful moving companies in the US was founded by two friends who wanted to do things differently.

They named their company "College Hunks Hauling Junk," (a good way to get attention), and then built an identity-based culture that starts with the name, Hunks, and is incorporated at every level of the organization.

While the name implies that hunky, attractive young men will be arriving to handle your moving boxes and heavy furniture, at this company, being a HUNK is more of a lifestyle.

Hunks take their name to heart:
- **H**onest
- **U**niformed
- **N**ice
- **K**nowledgeable
- **S**ervice

To be a Hunk is to embody the identity of the HUNKS—with every employee promising to be courteous, friendly, and respectful of your belongings.

One of their core values is "always branding," which means to always strive for positivity, community-oriented service, and delivering 100-percent client satisfaction with every job. Their culture is embodied by the identity of the organization and is present in everything from their core values to their customer service. The company is transparent about their culture, featuring a page of "funny questions" they get asked on their website.

These questions include things like: "Are they all really hunks?" "Are they all really in college?" or "You must do a lot of work on college campuses at the end of semesters, right?"

Instead of your typical FAQs, College Hunks Hauling Junk uses these questions to be self-deprecating. They acknowledge the common misconceptions and reassert their commitment to being fun, having great customer service, and living out their core values.

IDENTITY GONE WRONG

The identity-based culture of College Hunks is a stark contrast to the looks-based hiring practices of clothing company Abercrombie & Fitch. In 2004, the preppy brand was hit with a class-action lawsuit alleging racial, ethnic, and appearance-based discrimination.

The lawsuit revealed the company's "Look Policy," that dictated specific physical characteristics employees were required to have, including weight, hairstyle, and clothing in order to represent the brand. The CEO at the time, Mike Jeffries, added fuel to the fire when he made statements calling the brand intentionally "exclusionary" and saying it was only designed for "cool, attractive" people.

The company settled in 2005 for fifty-million dollars and agreed to implement new, more inclusive and diverse hiring policies. They were also required to hire a VP of diversity to drive more inclusive practices.[49]

Abercrombie & Fitch's attempt to create an identity was misplaced, offensive, and ultimately illegal. This stems from a company culture that's rooted in poor leadership and a complete lack of marketing strategy or understanding.

An identity-based culture should always be a positive force, opening up more seats at your organization's table. A culture that's based on one perspective or experience is too limited to translate to anything useful, desirable, or aspirational.

IMPROVE YOUR IDENTITY-BASED CULTURE

A strong culture that drives the identity you want your organization and team members to adopt always starts with your core values or non-negotiables.

Make sure you know *why* you want your people to show up and serve in a specific way before you ask them to do it. When you have core values to back an identity-based culture, it's easier to get buy-in from your workers.

Give serious consideration to your existing core values or newly-selected non-negotiables to make sure they support the identity you're inviting your entire organization to adopt. Enhance the way you want your organization to be known.

Conclusion and Invitation

Welcome to the official conclusion of this book.

Before you go, there's something important we need to take care of first.

At the beginning, I invited you to embrace your identity as a Marketer. You opened your mind, accepted that we are all marketers in our own rights, and entertained your own calling to be something more.

You became a Marketer in the opening pages, but now?

Now that you have read through these chapters, learned what Identity Marketing is, and how powerful it can be, and worked through the Identity Code framework to apply the principles to your own life, you've earned an upgrade.

No longer simply a Marketer—I dub thee, Rainmaker.

You're not just a Rainmaker in your business or work, either. You're ready to make it rain, have fun, and be radically open to growth and learning at home, in your relationships with others, and in your relationship with yourself.

You are well equipped to practice the art and science of ethical persuasion, helping people get out their own way and pursue what they truly want and who they aspire to be.

It's time to make it rain!

Now that you have officially upgraded your identity, it's time to embrace the Rainmaker code of values, ethics, and beliefs.

Rainmakers:

- Adhere to a higher standard of ethical marketing, rejecting manipulative tactics outright.

- Own their role as the *boss*. I believe there's a Veyoncé inside each and every one of us—you just have to free yourself up to accepting and championing this version of yourself.

- Aren't afraid to try new things, because we don't believe in failure. Everything we do is an experiment, and every outcome we achieve helps us learn something.

- Help other Rainmakers. We don't see others as our competition—we're here to seriously cheer one another on and practice abundant generosity with our skills, expertise, love, and support.

- Are here to COMPETE! We love a good challenge, and we show up for our battles with confidence and joy.

We are a breed of our own, completely in love with the idea that our ideas, perceptions, and perspectives can help others get closer to who they want to be.

When we don't channel our energy positively, it's easy to become burned-out shells of ourselves.

So take care, Rainmaker. Balance your zeal for success and commitment to showing up with the same amount of rest and true relaxation.

We've learned from so many examples of companies, big and small, but now it's your turn to make everything in this book work for you.

It's time to move from learning into active expansion—embodying your own upgraded identity to make a bigger impact and lead your buyers toward the best version of themselves.

As you leave the pages of this book and go back into the real world, it's easy to get lost in the weeds of business, marketing, leadership, and life. Don't lose your ability to experiment, to try and see. Hold your marketing loosely, so it has room to breathe, evolve, and grow.

Thank you for joining me on this journey to and through Identity Marketing. For so long, I was on this path alone: navigating my way, breaking through barriers only to be met with yet another obstacle, and feeling like I might never find my way through.

It's such an honor to have not only put this book in your hands, but to have walked with you on this Identity Marketing path.

You know who you are. Now go show the world.

Your ocean is calling!

I'll be right here, cheering you on every step of the way.

Additional Resources

Welcome to your Identity Marketing tool box! Here we are sharing all the resources and tools we've created to help you put what you just read and learned into ACTION.

You can find everything you need at ***identitymarketingbook.com.***

There you'll find:

- An invitation to the Identity Marketing Intensive—the *best* way to get hands-on support and guidance as you work through the Identity Code framework with our team of identity coaches.

- Downloadable worksheets and guides to keep you on track as you implement your new marketing identity.

- The audio-book format of *Identity Marketing* if you want to relisten and expand your learning.

Don't let this be an awesome book you read and then leave to gather dust on your bookshelf.

Take what you've learned and USE it! That's what Rainmakers do.

Acknowledgments

This book began with a single word — *identity*. I didn't enter 2024 planning to write a book, but in the midst of my sister's breast cancer journey, I felt an undeniable impression that I couldn't ignore.

The word stayed with me, so I wrote it on my bathroom mirror, not knowing what it meant but trusting it would unfold in time. Slowly, through reflection and revelation, that one word became the foundation of ideas, action, and ultimately this book. I am deeply grateful for the divine inspiration and guidance that carried me through this journey and helped me co-create this profound body of work.

Thanks to my family (my dreamy husband, endlessly energetic man cubs, and crazy Cubans) for always believing in me, giving me the space I need to execute my big dreams, and being there with a word of affirmation or a big hug whenever I need it. You guys are always it for me.

ACKNOWLEDGEMENTS | 285

Let it be known that I could never have turned all my thoughts, inspiration, meticulous research, and big ideas into a clear, engaging book without my writing partner, Emily Conley. I'm not exaggerating when I say that this book would never have happened without you. Thanks for trusting me and believing that together we could figure out this whole "writing a book thing." Turns out, we're pretty freaking good at it—and wicked fast!

Many thanks to the number of experts who lent their advice, expertise, and feedback along the winding road of self-publishing my first book ever – Jillian Garvin Durkin, Josh Bernoff, Nick Pavlidis, and Alexandra Franzen.

To my team, the V-hive: You guys are simply the best. You have each been willing to learn and grow, to try new crazy things when I think them up, and make sure we only deliver the best results out there. You all work at the speed of light, and I'm pretty sure we get more done in a week than most teams get done in a month.

And to every CEO, marketer, business owner, and leader who shared your story, sat down with me on my podcast, sent me a Voxer, or gave so generously of your time and experience—thank you, thank you, thank you!

To all of my former clients and employers: your leadership, creativity, and stories have been a constant source of inspiration. The lessons I learned working alongside you and the challenges we tackled together helped shape the ideas in this book. Thank you for giving me the experiences that ultimately taught me what it truly means to be an ethical marketer.

To the marketers who inspire me: Seth Godin, Donald Miller, Ann Handley, Nancy Harhut, April Dunford, Jay Baer, Andrew Davis, Jay Acunzo, Michael Barber, Tamsen Webster, Alex Cattoni, and Gary Vaynerchuk—your groundbreaking work, daring ideas, and tireless efforts have paved the way for everything I and fellow marketers have accomplished. This book is as much a tribute to your brilliance as it is a new step forward in the journey you began.

No big dream is ever accomplished alone. I'm eternally grateful to everyone who played a part—big or small—in bringing this book to life.

ACKNOWLEDGEMENTS

About the Author

For Veronica Romney, marketing is the art and science of ethically persuading someone to say "yes" to what you have to offer. The daughter of Cuban immigrants, Romney grew up with an entrepreneurial spirit and a fascination for human beings, how we define our identities, and what motivates us to act.

With over seventeen years of experience as marketer, giving keynote speeches, facilitating workshops, and strategically consulting with top performers, Veronica's mission is to empower marketing teams to not only perform better and generate record-breaking revenue results, but to also reignite their passion for their work, fostering a culture of proactivity and long-term commitment within their companies.

When she's not helping audiences and private clients "make it rain," you can find Veronica hosting the weekly *Rainmaker Podcast* and wrangling her two man cubs among the beautiful oak trees of North Carolina.

ABOUT THE AUTHOR | *289*

Notes

NOTES FOR CHAPTER 1

1. "Harley-Davidson Custom Caskets." Sky Caskets. Accessed December 11, 2024. https://skycaskets.com/custom-caskets/harley-davidson/.

   "Harley-Davidson Road King Hearse." Motorcycle Funerals Accessed December 11, 2024. https://motorcyclefunerals.com/harley-davidson-road-king.

2. Bernard Vandermeersch and Ofer Bar-Yosef, "The Paleolithic Burials at Qafzeh Cave, Israel," *Paléo*, no. 30–1 (2019): 256–75. Research Gate. https://doi.org/10.4000/paleo.4848.

3. "Ohio man Bill Standley buried astride Harley-Davidson." *BBC News*, US & Canada. Last modified February 1, 2014. Accessed July 19, 2024. https://www.bbc.com/news/world-us-canada-25987743.

NOTES FOR CHAPTER 2

4. Americus Reed and Mark Forehand (editors), *Handbook of Research on Identity Theory in Marketing* (Publishing House, 2019). 2.

NOTES FOR CHAPTER 3

5. Edelman. "2022 Edelman Trust Barometer." Accessed July 24, 2024. https://www.edelman.com/trust/2022-trust-barometer.

   PowerReviews. "Power of Reviews Survey 2021." Accessed July 24, 2024. https://www.powerreviews.com/power-of-reviews-survey-2021/.

6. Romney, Veronica. Interview with Kelly Ruta for podcast episode (unaired). Recorded November 4, 2025. *The Rainmaker Podcast*.

NOTES FOR CHAPTER 4

7. Clear, James. *Atomic Habits*. (Publishing House, 2018). 30-31.

8. Clear, 2018, 31.

9. Kraus, Rachel. "I Don't Look 'Pretty' While Working Out, and That's Okay" *Well + Good*, Accessed July 24, 2024. https://www.wellandgood.com/pretty-while-working-out/.

NOTES FOR CHAPTER 5

10. Gerwig, Greta and Noah Baumbach(screenwriters). *Barbie*. Directed by Greta Gerwig. Warner Bros Pictures, HeyDey Films, LuckyChap Entertainment, NB/GG Pictures, Mattel Films. 2023.

11. Maglione, Liz and Nathan Baynard, "Barbie," The Gathering, 2023, Banff, Canada.

12. *Sports Illustrated* Swimsuit Edition. Volume 220, Issue 8. February 18, 2014.

13. Maglione and Baynard, 2023, Banff, Canada

14. Maglione and Baynard, 2023, Banff, Canada

NOTES FOR CHAPTER 6

15. "Travis Kelce confirms the Taylor Swift effect was real for his podcast: 'We were happy to have dog food sponsors, now we can pick and choose who we want'." *Yahoo Finance*. Accessed July 24, 2024. https://finance.yahoo.com/news/travis-kelce-reveals-taylor-swift-104925640.html.

16. Taylor Swift, "Taylor Swift - #VEVOCertified, Pt. 3: Taylor Talks About Her Fans." produced/published by Taylor Swift, October 29, 2012. YouTube. https://www.youtube.com/watch?v=ehLp0cjqkRk.

17. Crupi, Anthony. "NFL Ratings Report Card: Network Deliveries Continue to Climb." *Sportico*, October 30, 2023. https://www.sportico.com/business/media/2023/nfl-tv-ratings-report-cbs-fox-nbc-1234701217/.

18. Adgate, Brad. "The NFL (and Travis Kelce) Is Benefitting from the Taylor Swift Effect." *Forbes*, October 2, 2023. https://www.forbes.com/sites/bradadgate/2023/10/02/the-nfl-and-travis-kelce-is-benefitting-from-the-taylor-swift-effect/.

19. Edison Research. "Welcome to New Heights: Taylor's Version." *Edison Research*, October 23, 2023. https://www.edisonresearch.com/press-release-welcome-to-new-heights-taylorsversion/.

NOTES FOR CHAPTER 7

20. Valens Research. "The Jump: Red Bull and GoPro Teamed Up for This Sky-High Marketing Stunt." *Valens Research*. Last updated April 30, 2020, accessed December 11, 2024. https://www.valens-research.com/dynamic-marketing-communique/the-jump-red-bull-and-gopro-teamed-up-for-this-sky-high-marketing-stunt-every-thursday-fyo/

21. Ede-Osifo, Uwa. "Five Things to Know About the Dallas Cowboy Cheerleaders and Their New Netflix Series." *The Dallas Morning News*, June 20, 2024. https://www.dallasnews.com/artsentertainment/2024/06/20/five-things-to-know-about-the-dallas-cowboy-cheerleaders-andtheir-new-netflix-series/.

22. McLeod, Saul. "Maslow's Hierarchy of Needs." *Simply Psychology*. Last updated January 24, 2024, accessed August 4, 2024. https://www.simplypsychology.org/maslow.html.

23. The Copy Posse - The New School of Copywriters. https://copyposse.com/

NOTES FOR CHAPTER 8

24. Original Instagram post by Nicole the Intern. https://www.instagram.com/p/C5tGVjXrwE8/

25. 270toWin. "1984 Presidential Election." Accessed December 11, 2024. https://www.270towin.com/1984_Election/.

NOTES FOR CHAPTER 8

26. https://www.maha.vote/

NOTES FOR CHAPTER 9

27. Convery, Alex, (screenwriter). *Air*. Directed by Ben Affleck. Amazon Studios, Skydance Sports, Artists Equity, Mandalay Pictures. 2023.

28. Miller, Julie. "Air: The Real Sonny Vaccaro on Matt Damon, Michael Jordan, and Shoe-Biz Heartbreak," *Vanity Fair*, April 7, 2023.

29. https://redantspants.com/blog/

30. Romney, Veronica. "The Original Female Workwear Pants and A Red Ant Colony Identity with Sarah Calhoun." *The Rainmaker Podcast*. October 21, 2024. https://www.veronicaromney.com/the-original-female-workwear-pants-and-a-red-ant-colony-identity-with-sarah-calhoun/

NOTES FOR CHAPTER 11

31. Harhut, Nancy, "How to Hack the Brains of Donors, Members, and Other Humans.," Direct Marketing Association of Washington, 2019. Washington D.C.

32. Scott, Missy. *Harley-Davidson Motor Company*. Greenwood Press, 2008. 43.

33. Romney, Veronica. Interview with Kierra Conover, "Why 1:1 Personalized Services are In and Scalable Group Programs Are Out," *The Rainmaker Podcast.* September 2, 2024, https://www.veronicaromney.com/why-11-personalized-services-are-in-and-scalable-group-programs-are-out-with-kierra-conover/.

34. Hamedy, Saba. "'Glee' finale: A Gleek's goodbye, and memories of how it all began." *Los Angeles Times,* March 23, 2015.

NOTES FOR CHAPTER 12

35. Hadland, Gracie. "The Toast of the Roast Comedian Nikki Glaser has been in the business for decades. But her set on the Tom Brady roast seems to have shifted something." *The Cut,* accessed December 11, 2024. https://www.thecut.com/article/nikki-glaser-tom-brady-roast.html.

36. Carvey, Dana and David Spade. "Nikki Glaser," *Fly on the Wall* podcast, May 15, 2024. https://podcasts.apple.com/us/podcast/nikki-glaser/id1603639502?i=1000655639889.

37. Google. "Google + Team USA – Dear Sydney", published by Google, July 26, 2024. YouTube. https://www.youtube.com/watch?v=NgtHJKn0Mck

NOTES FOR CHAPTER 13

38. Carmody, Dennis P., & Lewis, Michael. "Brain activation when hearing one's own and others' names." *Brain Research*, vol. 112, no. 1, 2007, pp. 78-86. https://www.sciencedirect.com/science/article/abs/pii/S0006899306022682?via%3Dihub.

39. Harhut, Nancy, "How to Hack the Brains of Donors, Members, and Other Humans.," Direct Marketing Association of Washington, 2019. Washington D.C.

40. Romney, Veronica, interview with Nicole Wingard, "Nicole the Intern: The Weight of Going Viral and Leading a 500k Army," *The Rainmaker Podcast*, September 30, 2024, https://www.veronicaromney.com/nicole-the-intern-the-weight-of-going-viral-and-leading-a-500k-army/.

41. https://copyposse.com/about.

42. One Day. https://www.teachforamerica.org/what-we-do/our-work.

NOTES FOR CHAPTER 15

43. Axon, Samuel. "Dell said return to the office or else—nearly half of workers chose 'or else'." *Ars Technica*, June 2024. https://arstechnica.com/gadgets/2024/06/nearly-half-of-dells-workforce-refused-to-return-to-the-office/.

44. Parker, Kim, Juliana Menasce Horowitz, and Rachel Minkin. "Majority of Workers Who Quit a Job in 2021 Cite Low Pay, No Opportunities for Advancement, Feeling Disrespected." *Pew Research Center*, March 9, 2022. https://www.pewresearch.org/shortreads/2022/03/09/majority-of-workers-who-quit-a-job-in-2021-cite-low-pay-no-opportunitiesfor-advancement-feeling-disrespected/.

45. Blind. "The Evolution of the Burnout: COVID-19 Edition." 2020. https://www.teamblind.com/blog/content/files/StateofBurnoutCovid19.pdf.

46. Innes, Molly. "CMO tenure falls to lowest level in more than a decade." *Marketing Week*. https://www.marketingweek.com/cmo-tenure-falls/.

NOTES FOR CHAPTER 16

47. Romney, Veronica. Interview with Ann Handley, "How Ann Handley Became the First Ever Chief Content Officer," *The Rainmaker Podcast*, September 9, 2024, https://www.veronicaromney.com/how-ann-handley-became-the-first-ever-chief-content-officer/

NOTES FOR CHAPTER 18

48. Reisner, Robert. "Nike's Tattooed Ekins." *The New York Times Magazine*, May 22, 1994. https://www.nytimes.com/1994/05/22/magazine/sunday-may-22-1994-nike-s-tattooed-ekins.html.

49. Lieff Cabraser Heimann & Bernstein, LLP. "Abercrombie Fitch Race Discrimination." Lieff, Cabraser, *Heimann & Bernstein, Attorneys at Law*. accessed September 29, 2024. https://www.lieffcabraser.com/employment/abercrombie-fitch/.